STOCK TRADING INVESTING FOR BEGINNERS

THE BIBLE FOR MAKING MONEY FROM HOME. HOW TO UNDERSTAND TRENDS AND LEARN NEW TECHNIQUES AND TACTICS. HOW THE MARKET WORKS WITH DAY TRADING AND FUTURES

Henry Anderson

Stock Trading Investing for Beginners

© Copyright 2020 by Henry Anderson

All rights reserved.

This document is geared towards providing exact and reliable information with regards to the topic and issue covered. The publication is sold with the idea that the publisher is not required to render accounting, officially permitted, or otherwise, qualified services. If advice is necessary, legal or professional, a practiced individual in the profession should be ordered.

From a Declaration of Principles which was accepted and approved equally by a Committee of the American Bar Association and a Committee of Publishers and Associations.
In no way is it legal to reproduce, duplicate, or transmit any part of this document in either electronic means or in printed format. Recording of this publication is strictly prohibited and any storage of this document is not allowed unless with written permission from the publisher. All rights reserved.

The information provided herein is stated to be truthful and consistent, in that any liability, in terms of inattention or otherwise, by any usage or abuse of any policies, processes, or directions contained within is the solitary and utter responsibility of the recipient reader. Under no circumstances will any legal responsibility or blame be held against the publisher for any reparation, damages, or monetary loss due to the information herein, either directly or indirectly.

Respective authors own all copyrights not held by the publisher. The information herein is offered for informational purposes solely, and is universal as so. The presentation of the information is without contract or any type of guarantee assurance.

The trademarks that are used are without any consent, and the publication of the trademark is without permission or backing by the trademark owner. All trademarks and brands within this book are for clarifying purposes only and are the owned by the owners themselves, not affiliated with this document.

Stock Trading Investing for Beginners

TABLE OF CONTENTS

INTRODUCTION 6

CHAPTER 1 HOW TO PICK OUT A BROKER 16

CHAPTER 2 STOCK PICKING STRATEGIES 21

CHAPTER 3 STOCK TRADING STRATEGIES 23

CHAPTER 4 BONDS 34

CHAPTER 5 DAY AND SWING TRADING 42

CHAPTER 6 FOREX TRADING 54

CHAPTER 7 OPTIONS TRADING 68

CHAPTER 8 HOW TO CREATE PASSIVE INCOME WITH DIVIDEND STOCKS 79

CHAPTER 9 FUNDAMENTALS OF INVESTING IN THE STOCK MARKET 92

CHAPTER 10 MINDSET 105

CHAPTER 11 RULES THAT HELP TO REDUCE YOUR RISKS IN THE STOCK MARKET 120

CHAPTER 12 THE HISTORY OF THE STOCK MARKET 128

CHAPTER 13 WHY YOU SHOULD INVEST IN STOCKS 148

CHAPTER 14 PICKING OUT STOCKS TO INVEST IN 151

CHAPTER 15 BUYING YOUR FIRST STOCK 156

CHAPTER 16 OPTIONS TRADING 162

- **CHAPTER 17** SWING TRADING STRATEGIES 181
- **CHAPTER 18** FOREX STRATEGIES AND STRATEGIES FOR BEGINNERS 190
- **CHAPTER 19** SETTING YOUR FINANCIAL GOAL 208
- **CHAPTER 20** TECHNICAL ANALYSIS 213
- **CHAPTER 21** FUNDAMENTAL ANALYSIS STRATEGY 220
- **CHAPTER 22** CUTTING YOUR LOSSES 226
- **CHAPTER 23** TAKING YOUR PROFITS 231
- **CHAPTER 24** MANAGING YOUR MONEY 237
- **CHAPTER 25** DIVERSIFICATION 250
- **CONCLUSION** 256

Introduction

The majority of the public do not understand what the stock market is. We've seen movies about it, but most of them were made simpler for us regular folks to understand. You cannot start investing not knowing what company stocks are and what their purpose is.

The first rule in any kind of investing is to "invest in what you know". In this chapter, we will discuss what the stock market really is and why every free market society has one.

What is the stock market?
The stock market is the overall platform in which people and organizations buy and sell stocks. Most developed country has at least one stock exchange. The stock exchange is a private company that manages and maintains the stock market. They provide the technology and the people needed to allow transactions to happen in the market. Put simply, the stock market is where you buy and sell stocks.

You may be asking, what exactly are stocks?

Stocks (also called equities or shares) are units that represent a person's claim to a company's assets and earnings. Companies sell these units to raise funds. The people who buy them are called stockholders (or shareholders). By selling stocks, companies give these investors a claim for their assets and future earnings.

Why does the stock market exist?

The stock market is an important part of the economy. To understand why it is necessary, you could put yourself in the shoes of the different stakeholders in the market.

First, you have the companies selling the stocks. They need the stock market to raise funds. The funds that they raise can be used for a number of growth-oriented business activities. For instance, the money could be used to develop more production assets. Increased production could lead to higher profits and this could increase the overall value of the company. The stock market could allow these companies to grow at a rate that may not be possible otherwise.

Next, we have the policy makers and the government in general. People in the government use the stock market and other investment markets as a litmus test for the economy. When consumers are in the mood for buying stocks and other securities, this may be an indicator that many people have money to spare. This is a good sign for the government because it shows that people have more money than they need for their basic needs. The activities in the stock market is also one of the factors that policy makers use when deciding to implement new financial policies. Policies such as printing new money and changing the Federal Interest

Rate are heavily dependent on the activities of investors in the market.

Lastly, we have the investors. When you start investing your money, you become a part of this group. The stock market allows you and other regular people to invest in the companies that you are familiar with. In the process, you aid the growth of the economy and if done right, you may be able to grow your money.

How was the stock market formed?

The stock market was not formed in a day. No one person invented it. Instead, it was formed over the centuries of people practicing mercantilism. The first stock market could be credited to the Dutch in the 1600s. While they are the first in recorded history to actually facilitate the sale of company stocks, the way may have been paved by the Italians who began selling other types securities as early as the 13th century.

At around this time, the governments of Venice, Pisa, Verona, Florence and many other city states worked with banks to sell government bonds to raise government funds. This was followed by the actual selling of company shares. However, there is no record stating that there is a formal meeting place for the sales of these shares. The stock certificates were bought and sold in person or through banks. They were also bought and sold among people who knew each other and were not generally available to the public.

It wasn't until the 1600s that the first marketplace for selling these unique types of securities first emerged.

It was at this time that the Dutch East India Company offered its company stocks to the public. Their company stocks were sold in the Amsterdam Exchange.

While today's trading experience uses computers and other digital tools, in the past, it was all done through ledgers and certificates. The stockholders of a company were written in a ledger. They are also given stock certificates as a receipt that they can show as proof that they are indeed stock holders.

In the United States, the earliest record of an organized exchange can be traced to the Buttonwood Agreement in the late 1700s. This agreement set the stage for the creation of the New York Stock Exchange (NYSE). The NYSE is the largest stock exchange in the world today. However, it started out as a small exchange that only traded government bonds. The first company stocks to be traded in the exchange were those of banks.

As the market grew, so did the exchange that managed it. In the past, the trades were done in tables in the streets and in coffee shops around New York. The exchange transferred its location multiple times before it settled in the now-iconic 11 Wall Street, Lower Manhattan, New York City, New York.

How did it develop to what it is today?

The evolution of Wall Street is closely connected with the development of communication technology. In the early days, only people around New York knew about the stock market and only the rich had the resources and the manpower to keep track of price changes in the market. People from other parts of the United States could not participate in the market unless they sent a representative to the exchange.

Everything changed with the development of the telegraph machine. With the help of this tool, people from far and wide were able to learn the stock prices sooner. This allowed investors from other parts of the country to participate in the market.

The development of other communication tools further increased access to the market. As the telephone became more common, it became one of the primary ways to connect with the market. Investors often talked with their brokers through the phone. They called their brokers to give transactional instructions.

The stock market was also one of the earliest industries to make use of the internet as a practical business tool. It all started when the National Association of Securities Dealers Automated Quotations (NASDAQ) provided digitalized priced quotes. This made it easier for investors and other market participants to keep track of market activities.

With the internet becoming more popular in the 90s, it was just a matter of time before it was used as a trading tool. In 1994, the company K. Aufhauser & Company, Inc. offered the first online trading platform.

Today, modern brokerages allow investors to do their own trades. They no longer needed to connect with a broker. Instead, investors can now place orders or stop existing orders through their online browser-based accounts.

Now that you have an idea about the stock market and your role in it, let's talk about what you need to get started.

What can the stock market do for you?

As you may already know, the stock market is one of the best ways to make money. There are two general ways that you can use to make your money in the stock market grow. First, you can increase the value of your money by earning dividends. Dividends are cash rewards that the company pays its investors. The dividends usually come from excess company profits and the amount that you will get depends on the number of shares that you own of a particular company.

The second way to earn using the stock market is through buying and selling stocks. This method is called capital appreciation. In this method, you buy the stocks and sell them later on when the price of the stocks increase. This is how most participants in the stock market make money.

Can you invest in it as a side job?

Investing directly in the stock market requires a certain degree of commitment. You can successfully invest by allocating only 5-8 hours a day to it. You will spend most of this time exploring the options in the stock market, studying charts and designing your trading approaches and strategies.

While you can do most of these things when the market is closed, it's best to focus on the market when it is open. You can integrate the activities of checking the events in the market and checking the performance of your current investing positions to your daily work activities.

To answer the question above, you can do it as a side job, but make sure that you do due diligence when investing. Take the time to study the companies you are looking to invest on.

You may also need to adjust your personal strategy based on the amount of time that you can spend on the market. If you have more time to spend, you can take active trading decisions. This is a type of trading where in you buy and sell your positions after a few days or weeks. You cannot take the same types of positions when you cannot keep your eyes on the market.

If you can only spend a small amount of time per week on the stock market on the other hand, it's best to choose long term positions when investing. Long term positions focus on trades that take months or even years to compete.

There are thousands of companies available on the stock market, but not all of them will provide you with a good return on investment. Some will provide you with one of the best opportunities to make money without all the risk and others will be failures right from the beginning. As a beginner, you may be worried about how you will sort these out so that you can pick the right stocks to make the most money for you.

The first thing that you should look at when you are ready to join the stock market is that you should never just pick out a stock, no matter what the circumstances are, simply because you heard through the grapevine or from a friend of a friend that the stock was a good one. Doing your own research is important. You can take the advice of other people, such as friends who are in the stock market and your broker, but remember that this is your investment and you need to be the one in control of it. Do some of your own research on the market, and you will soon learn which stocks are the best ones for your needs, regardless of what other people say.

If you have already done some research and have come up with a list of companies that you want to look at some more and possibly invest in, make sure to take some time searching on their website. Most of them will have information about their stocks, and this can be helpful when making your decision. You need to take a look at all of their reports on finances if possible to because this tells you how the company has done so far on the market. You will be surprised at how much information you are able to get about a company just by snooping around a little bit.

While there are a lot of things that you will need to consider when it comes to picking out a stock to work with, you need to go with one that will actually make you money in the process. Never pick a stock that is obviously going to cost you more than you can earn and try to go with the ones that are winners. There are a few things that you can take a look at to limit your risks including:

- The margin of profit for that company.
- The debts that a company has and how much those debts are.
- The return on equity with that company.
- The debt to equity ratio. This is a good thing to look up because it will give you an idea of how this particular company spends their money and whether they do so responsibly or not.
- How the company has done in the past and whether they are expected to do the same, better, or worse.

What should I be looking for?

So, you may be curious about what things you need to look for to pick out a good company to invest in. You will want to spend some time looking through charts and graphs to see how a particular stock has been doing inside the stock market, but that is only one part of the story. You also need to take a look at the company itself to see if it will maintain that status for the long term. For example, there may be a company who looks good when you go through the charts and graphs, but if they are not good at spending money or keeping their debts down, then they are not the company for you. Some of the different things that you should consider looking at when you are ready to pick out a stock includes:

Who manages the business?

This is one of the first things that you should look at when you want to start investing in a company. Who manages the business will help you to figure out how the company is doing now as well as how it will do in the future. Many beginners consider the management of a company not all that important. However, if the current management is not doing well with running the company, even a solid company can go downhill fast.

Now, you need to carefully consider the management of a company before you decide to invest in it. There are a few points that you can consider such as what the return on equity is if the shareholders are still earning a profit each year. If the equity return of the company is five percent or higher, it is usually a safe bet that the company will keep growing and doing well. Also, look and see how the management is doing with others and with each other. Are they getting along and making decisions that are good for the company, or is there are a lot of internal fighting that could ruin the company?

Chapter 1 How to Pick Out a Broker

As a beginner, you will find that working with a broker is a great idea. Your broker will be able to answer your questions, discuss your trading strategy with you, and can even offer the platform that you will use to get the trading done. This is a great way in order to ensure that you are set up for success as much as possible right from the beginning.

There are many different types of brokers that you can choose to work with and it may be worth your time to talk to several and see what they offer in terms of costs, advice, and more. You don't want to run into any problems or surprises with your broker after you have already agreed to sign up with them. Many brokers can help you out with your investment, but you may need to sit down with a few and discuss your options and then compare your notes before picking just one.

When you talk to a potential broker, you must make sure that you fully understand any of their fees ahead of time. The first thing to consider is how much you plan to utilize the services of a particular broker. If you plan to just use their platform and do most of the work on your own, then the cost of your broker is going to be less. If you are an absolute beginner and you need someone who will be willing to walk you through the process, help you out with the trades, answer your questions, and be there to guide you, then that broker is going to cost a bit more.

So, the first thing that you must look at is how much of the trading you want to do on your own compared to how much help you think you will need. You can always get more help, but it is going to come at a cost, and this can eat into any profits that you might make on the market. It might be nice to hire a broker who can walk you through all the steps and be there in order to help you out, but if that ends up eating all of the profits that you are earning, then why even be in the stock market?

As a beginner, you also probably don't want to try to do all of the trading on your own. Yes, this will save you a good deal of money, but then you are on your own. More experienced traders like to work in this manner. It allows them to experiment, bring in some of their own tools that they have seen as successful, and they can save money. But most of the investors who decide to do things this way have been in the market for some time and have learned the ropes that are needed to keep things organized and working smoothly.

Most beginners will want to work with something in between. They need some help as they are learning and they don't want to do things completely on their own, but it can save money and be a good learning experience to do some of the work on their own. Finding someone who is willing to answer your questions and give you advice when you need it can be a great benefit of a broker, but this doesn't mean that you need or want them to do everything for you. Experiment, interviewing, and talking to various brokers can help you find the one who offers the best service, along with the best price, around.

The next thing you need to look at is the type of fees that your broker asks for. Some brokers will ask for a set fee each month or year. This is the amount that everyone who uses this broker is going to need to pay when they first get started. This can be beneficial if you are doing a lot of trades, such as day trading, each week because you won't have to worry about being charged extra for all the different trades that you do. It can also be nice because you won't have to worry about how much you make in profits because the amount is the same no matter what.

Other brokers will charge based on how much you earn on each trade. This is a great option to go with in the beginning because you probably aren't earning all that much in profits. In the beginning, being charged a fixed rate may sound reasonable, but depending on how much you actually bring in on each trade or in dividends for the first year, you may find that the flat rate eats up a good percentage of any profits that you earn.

There are also some brokers who will charge a fee based on how many times you enter and exit a trade. For those who go with a long-term investing strategy and plan to take out dividends each quarter, but who don't plan to get into new trades that often, this is a great option to choose. You only have to pay for the trades that you do; for long-term investors, there aren't that many trades.

With this final option, there can be some issues for day traders. If you are doing a minimum of one trade (and often more) each day, then this can start to add up pretty quickly. If you have to pay for each of those trades, even a small amount, it is going to add up and take up a lot of the profits that you are earning. And since day trading and other similar methods don't necessarily earn a ton for each trade (the money comes with earning a little profit on a lot of trades), working with this kind of commission plan isn't the best.

With all of these different fee structures and options, it is hard to know which one is the best for you to go with. Before you even start to look for an available broker, it is important that you come up with the investment strategy that you want to work with. Do you think that you will need a lot of help with your trades or would you rather do a lot of it on your own? Do you think that you will want to be a day trader or more of a long-term trader? Are there any other special circumstances that you may need to look at before deciding on the best broker for you?

And before we move on, make sure that you check out all the different features that your broker is going to offer. Each broker is going to have their own platform that you can use to access the stock market and do your trades. They all have different features, different charts, and more. Some brokers will even let you check out their platform before you decide to work with them; if they do, take advantage of it. You may find that after talking to a few brokers, there may be one that has more of the features you need or want when compared to all the others.

Your broker is going to be a great tool to work with when you are ready to join the stock market. They will provide you with what you need: the platform, the tools and features, and even some suggestions and advice. Finding one you can trust and ask questions of can make a bit difference in the amount of success you see with stock market investing.

Chapter 2 Stock Picking Strategies

While it comes to the accumulation of wealth and personal finance, some subjects are a bit more talked as compared to stocks. It is simple to figure out why: playing with a stock market is quite thrilling. However, on the financial roller-coaster, everyone wants to experience some thrilling ups in the absence of downs.

There're nearly six-thousand traded firms in the United States. It shows a 37 percent decrease in the number of American-listed firms since 1997. What should an investor choose?

Tested Strategies

In the article, we will examine some most important time-tested strategies to find good stocks (at least trying to avoid bad ones). We will learn the stock-picking art relying on a specific set of criteria, to get a return rate that's above the market's average.

Some are easy: for instance, The Dogs of the Dow strategy is very easy that this takes a couple of minutes to understand how the whole system does work. Value investing and growth are quite complicated, and these kinds of investors need to invest time to understand financial ratios, valuation, to name a few.

Being Patient

Patience is undoubtedly a virtue while this comes to investment – in terms of patiently waiting for the appropriate time for entering a position, and waiting for a while until you have done all of the homework before making your very first investment. The chances of success would enhance greatly when you know very well about what you are doing.

A lot of long-term investors generally use the fundamental analysis for finding out possible chances. When you are interested in understanding these methods, learn fundamental analysis that would teach you the tools and strategies used by the successful investment experts. You would learn how to analyze cash flow and income statements, spot weak points in a balance sheet of the stock, and also use different valuation ratios for comparing opportunities in different on-demand video, interactive content, and exercises.

Chapter 3 Stock Trading Strategies

You cannot achieve a consistent flow of profits just by relying on luck. To significantly increase your chances of success, you should use effective strategies. Take note that just reading about these strategies is not enough. Investing in stocks is like learning a new skill. You also need to practice it. Let us discuss some of the notable strategies that you should know:

Fundamental analysis

Fundamental analysis is also referred to as the 'lifeblood' of investment. Hence, this is definitely something that is worth learning. This strategy does not just apply to the stock market but also in all kinds of investment. So, what is fundamental analysis? Fundamental analysis studies the fundamentals or the basics. As such, it is very important. You are probably familiar with the saying, "Knowledge is power." Well, this is what this strategy is all about. When you use this strategy, you should research and analyze the different factors that affect a stock or the stock market in general, such as the economy, level of competition, legalities, as well as market acceptance, among other things.

When you use this strategy, it is important that you follow up on the latest news since the news reveals important information about the stock market. Although fundamental analysis might be the strategy that demands the most time and effort, it is also highly effective. If you are serious about being a successful stock investor, then you should definitely learn about this strategy. In fact, successful investors use this daily. As a professional investor, you need to be up-to-date with the latest developments in the stock market.

It is also worth noting that fundamental analysis can be used along with another strategy. This strategy is not just about gathering all kinds of information. Rather, it has to be high-quality and reliable information. Of course, you also need to do your own analysis to identify the best information. You will soon realize that the more that you know about the market and the different stocks, the more likely it is that you will come up with the right investment decisions.

Technical analysis

If you are the visual type of person, then you might find this strategy interesting. Technical analysis makes use of graphs and charts to study the price movements of a particular stock. The idea behind this strategy is that the different factors that can affect a stock have their final effect on its price. Therefore, just by analyzing the price movements of a stock, you also get to deal with all the factors that influence it. You might want to consider this as the simplified and visual version of fundamental analysis.

When you use this strategy, you should learn to read patterns. Okay, you might be wondering: "Do patterns really exist?" The answer is 'yes.' In fact, even a random generator creates patterns. However, it should be noted that patterns come and go. What this means is, you cannot expect to see a pattern all of the time. There will be times when no matter how hard you study a graph, there is simply no pattern to be seen. Again, you don't need to worry because this is normal. A common mistake is forcing yourself to see a pattern even when no pattern exists. Remember, always make your analysis with a clear and unbiased mind. It is better for you not to proceed with making a decision than forcing yourself to see something which isn't even there.

Just like fundamental analysis, technical analysis can be used together with another strategy. In fact, many expert traders use both fundamental and technical analysis at the same time. Indeed, the more information that you have, the more likely it is that you can come up with the right investment decision. Technical analysis is an excellent strategy for short-term investments, but it can also be used for long-term investments.

Examples of technical analysis

The technical analysis foresees that the price continues to bounce on the trend lines as in the figure above until it breaks a support as in the figure below to accelerate sharply. These are great times to enter the market.

Averaging down

This strategy will allow you to purchase stocks at a bargain. You can then sell them for profit. The best way to explain how this works is by using an example. Let us say, you want to buy the stocks of company X, and its current price is $10 per stock. You then make a buy order at the said rate. If its price increases, then you can easily sell it for profit. Now, if the price decreases, then according to this strategy, you should make another buy order. So, if the price drops, say, to $9, then you should make a buy order at $9. Now, if the price decreases again, then make another buy order at the lower price. This way you are buying stocks at a much lower price.

Okay, you might be wondering: "Are you not simply buying a losing stock?" Although it may look like it, this is not actually the case. In fact, you are making a sound investment. Just imagine how much profit you could make once the price of the stock goes back to its original price (its price when you first applied the strategy) or higher. All the buy orders that you have made will give you a nice return on your initial investment.

Now, it should be noted that this approach is considered highly aggressive, so be very careful every time you use it. The key here is to identify a stock that will most likely increase in price. Take as much time as you can to research the stock concerned, as your success will depend on whether its price will increase or at least recover in the near future.

A good strategy to use together with averaging down is fundamental analysis or technical analysis. You cannot use averaging down alone on its own as it relates only to the amount that you invest and does not tell you where to make an investment. Of course, where you put your money in is a crucial factor when it comes to making profitable investments. This strategy will allow you to weather fluctuations in the market since you're holding on to profitable stock investments. Again, keep in mind that although this seems highly practical, it is still considered a highly aggressive approach.

Growth investing

This is where you invest in the stocks of a company because you believe that the company has a potential to grow. This is usually used for small and start-up companies since they have room for development. When you use this strategy, take a look at new businesses. Consider how they are positioned in the market. Can they match up with the competition? Do not just focus on the company. Keep in mind that the strengths and weaknesses of a business are relative to the strengths and weaknesses of its competitors. Therefore, you should also keep an eye on competing businesses. This is a good way to gauge how a particular business is doing in the market. It is not enough that a company has space to grow, but the business should take positive actions to grow even further. Last but not the least, you should also pay attention to market acceptance. After all, no matter how amazing a business is, it would not do any good if the market ignores it or simply does not accept what it offers. These are the important things to consider when you use this strategy. The drawback of using this strategy is that since you will most likely be dealing with start-up companies, there may not be enough information that you could use to measure the profitability of these companies. This is a challenge that you have to overcome with this strategy.

Value investing

This is similar to growth investing. However, in this case, it is the value that you need to look into. When you use this strategy, you should look for a company that offers its stocks at a price that is lower than their actual value. Okay, this is where the challenge is. It is you who will have to determine the value of their stocks of the company. You need to look for stocks that are underpriced in the market. The idea behind this strategy is that the value of the stocks will soon adjust and correct itself. When this happens, and if you find a company that is underpriced, then you will soon gain a nice profit. Unlike growth investing, value investing does not just work on new companies. It can also apply to old companies or stocks. Still, this is a good strategy to use on new and start-up companies since they tend to have good value but have a low stock price. It is good to use this strategy together with fundamental analysis. Take as much time as you need to study the company. Of course, do not forget to compare its strengths and weaknesses with the strengths and weaknesses of its competitors. If you find a company that has good value but is underpriced, then that is an opportunity that you can take advantage of. When you use this approach, it is important that you should not be biased about anything. Always keep an open mind and do your best to understand the company before you make any real investment.

Stock split

In a 'stock split,' a stock is split, and so it gets divided. For example, if a stock or share costs $40. After a stock split, then you will end up with two stocks at $20 each. Take note that it does not always have to be an equal split. The point is that the stock will be divided, and so its price should also be divided accordingly. This is usually done by companies when the price of its shares gets too high. So, they move for a stock split to lower the price. This is also because investors tend to shy away from stocks that are too pricey. Now, this is actually a good sign. It usually means that the business is doing good. Normally, after a stock split, the price of stocks still continues to increase. When you use this strategy, you should pay attention to companies that just declared a stock split. This normally signifies that they're doing well.

Now, you should be careful. A common mistake is to fall for a reverse split. This is like a stock split, but it is not good. In a reverse split, stocks are combined, which causes the price of stocks to increase. Since there is an increase in price, it might look as if it were a good investment, although that is not really the case. Here is an example. Let us say that there are 10 stocks at $10 each. In case of a reverse split, then you will end up with five stocks at $20 each. This is the opposite of a reverse split. In this case, the price of stocks increases not because the company is doing well, but it's because of a manipulative action made by the company. Hence, do not forget that a simple increase in the price of stocks is not good enough of an indicator that the company is doing well.

Take note that, although a stock split is often a good indication that the company is doing well, you should still do your own research before you make an investment. A stock split alone is not enough. You should take a closer look at the company and study it carefully. This way you can increase the chances of making a good investment.

Stock mastery

The more that you know and understand a particular stock, the more likely that you can predict its price movement. This is the idea behind this strategy. When you use this approach, you should choose a particular stock that you like which you think is profitable. Your job is to make sure that you read and analyze the said stock every day. After some time, you will notice that since you know the said stock so well already, you can easily predict its behavior in the market, and this will allow you to take advantage of it and make a nice profit.

Read and find out as much as you can about your chosen stock. Now, it is also common that you might suddenly realize that the stock is not a profitable investment as you study it. This is well and good because it will help you lower your losses. In this case, do not be discouraged. Simply move to another stock and start over. Do not consider your efforts as a waste. If you end up with a losing stock, then be thankful for the fact that you have saved money by not making any real investment.

Once you gain mastery over a stock, then you can start taking advantage of it. But, how do you know if you have mastered a particular stock? There is no strict rule regarding this matter. The important thing is that you can predict its price movements correctly most of the time. Once you attain mastery over a particular stock, then feel free to master another stock. The more stocks that you get to master, the better chances you have of making a large profit. Do not rush the process of learning and researching information about a particular stock. Take note that you are aiming for mastery, and not just having mere knowledge of a stock.

Develop your own

As a professional investor, you can develop your own strategy. It can be as simple as making a few adjustments to the strategies that you already know, but you are also free to come up with an entirely new strategy of your own. The life of a full-time investor is mostly about developing a strategy. Keep in mind that the stock market is a continuously moving market. The strategy that you use should be up to date with the latest changes and developments. Therefore, as you work on your strategy, you should also keep a close eye on the stock market.

Developing your own strategy can take a long time. Be ready to go through some trial and error before you adopt a strategy and apply it using real money. This is a good time to make use of the demo account provided by your stockbroker so that you can test your strategy in a real market environment without risking any real money. If you do not want to make use of the demo account, then you can simply make small investments and see how they go.

Take note that strategies are highly sensitive. This means that even a minor change in your strategy can make a big difference. Therefore, when it comes to developing your own strategy, be sure to test it more than once even if you only have to make a small adjustment.

Chapter 4 Bonds

Bonds have been in existence since time immemorial. They were used by ancient governments to raise money for various capital-intensive causes, which is the same use to which they are put even today. So what exactly are bonds? In the stock trading sense of the word, a bond is like a unit of a bigger loan that a company or government takes from a large pool of investors for a specific purpose. The whole loan, thus taken, also falls under the definition of a bond. What individual investors hold in their hands as the bond is usually the certificate given to signify the borrower/lender relationship they enter into with the borrower. In the bond certificate, the terms of payment and details of the loan are indicated, including the interest rate and maturity date. Trading in bonds can either be over the counter in the bourse or between lender and borrower.

How Bonds Work

The system of bond borrowing can be traced way back to the ancient Mesopotamian financial systems, where corporations borrowed grain with the promise to pay back the principal plus interest at a certain date. Instead of placing the company assets as surety, a bond was used instead, symbolizing the borrower's deepest commitment to repay the loan. This obligation to repay the debt became to represent the bond the current world knows as financial systems evolved. Bonds are necessitated by a number of realities that only the insider might know about the capital markets.

The capital requirements of large corporations are quite extensive. To start a new project, finance ongoing operations (especially in R & D), and repay old debts that have not been repaid yet, companies need to raise massive amounts of money. From large infrastructural projects to war efforts, governments have an appetite for capital that is tax remissions from citizens and businesses do not meet.

In some cases, the banks cannot meet the demand for these needs simply because the amount of money these entities require is so great. The risk of a bank going under in the event of these massive borrowers defaulting is too great, which means that corporations and governments have to become creative about how they raise the money for whatever their super-important need might be.

The way to do this is by distributing the risk to so many people that the effect of a possible default is blunted by the very fact that it is spread over many people. Having 10,000 people risk $1,000 each is preferable to one entity risking the $10,000,000 because the impact would be less serious on each person. With a single lender, such a huge default would definitely take the lender under.

Bonds are considered to be quite conservative as investment options, mostly because the possibility of losing one's money is way low. Short of going out of business, bond issuers repay their debt obligations in full, and even in the event of going bankrupt, bonds are treated as creditors and paid first from the liquefied assets of a company. Governments absolutely pay their bonds, sometimes issuing a new bond just to repay the old.

Characteristics of Bonds

While there are quite a number of types of bonds, some of their characteristics are uniform to them all. Understanding the characteristics and terminologies used to describe them is crucial to learning how to invest in them.

The *face value* is the principal amount that the issuer is expected to pay the holder of a bond when the period that has been agreed upon passes. The face value remains fixed over time even when the supply and demand drive the price up in the stock market. These external influences of the stock market determine whether the bond sells at a premium (higher than the face value) or a discount (lower than the price indicated on the bond certificate).

The *maturity*, of course, is the due date for the bond's principal. The issuer decides the maturity period for the bond, and the market responds by buying into the idea with their money. A lengthy maturity time increases the risk of nonrepayment, so the issuer has to promise a higher yield to entice investors.

At the time of issuing the bond, the borrower promises to pay a certain amount over the face value, which is otherwise known as the interest rate or the *yield/coupon.* The coupon is the equivalent of servicing a loan, with the borrower expected to pay a certain amount every year or semi-annually. This coupon could be fixed (which means that it never changes despite the state of the economy), or it could be adjustable, allowing the borrower to vary their coupon payment depending on certain market conditions.

Because their interest rates are either fixed or more rigid than the rest of the stock market, bonds are considered to be a safe haven for conservative investors during an economic crisis. Lower interest rates in the general economy drive the interest of a bond higher due to increased demand. The increased demand comes about because investors suddenly view bonds as being more profitable even if their price remains the same. Bond yield thus moves in an inverse direction with interest rates in the rest of the market— down when the former is high and high when it is low. Another factor that affects yield is the rate of inflation. With their low interest rates, bonds become attractive when the inflation rate is lower because the net yield increases. Short-term bonds that are expected to be exposed to a shorter period of inflation tend to have a lower interest rate while those with a longer maturity period (and thus risk) require a greater interest in recompense.

Based on the yield, we have several types of bonds. The common one is the coupon bond where the issuer pays a certain amount of money above the face value of a bond. Another type of bond is the zero-coupon type, which is issued at a discounted rate compared to the face value. When the bond matures, the bond is paid in full, and the investor makes their money that way. The United States treasury bills are traded as zero-coupon bonds, so a $100 note sells at, say, $98. At maturity, the inflation-adjusted interest rate will be around 2.5%.

Another type of bond is the convertible type. This one allows bondholders to take the decision to convert their bond principal and use it to buy stocks. The option to convert debt into equity when the share price reaches a certain level allows private bond issuers to reduce the coupon. The lowered interest rate at the point of issuance serves the company better as the project takes off, and the fact that the debt is converted into equity dilutes the stakes of other shareholders at no cost to the company. As for the investors, the convertible bond presents double insurance for their investment. If the share does not reach levels attractive for purchasing, the bond yield is still high enough to give a considerably good return. But the fact that they can convert the bond into stock at any time, at any stock price, means that the investor gets their pick of the best moments to buy shares, which could be very profitable.

A similar but somewhat different type of bond is the callable type that may be redeemed by the issuer at any point before the maturity. The callable bond allows the issuer to buy back the debt at lower interest rates and re-issue at a cheaper cost. Because issuers buy the bonds back when interest rates are in decline, it means that the bondholders are relieved of their bonds at just the point when the price is in an upward trajectory. For that reason, investors do not overly like callable bonds and opt for non-callable types when the coupon rate, maturity, and credit rating of the company is the same.

Bonds Issuers

The three main types of entities issue bonds are corporate, municipals, and governments. The government is the main bond issuer, responsible for more than 50% of all bonds floating around in the stock market. The treasury issues bonds on behalf of the government, with the word assigned to them varying by their maturity rate. Bonds that are expected to mature within the year are defined as bills, those that mature within ten years of being issued are known as notes, and those that are expected to mature ten to twenty years after their issue are known simply as bonds. The more conventional name for all three categories of government-issued bonds is treasuries. It is not uncommon to hear them all being referred to as treasury bills, treasury notes, and treasury bonds respectively. Local governments issue bonds to raise money for certain development projects. Because these bonds are unfamiliar and investors are often unsure whether the issuer can actually pay up, the coupon income is often specified as being tax-free in a bid to attract more investors.

Comparison with Stocks

The main difference between bonds and stocks is that stocks represent a stake in the business while a bond is essentially a credit service an investor extends to the company or the government. The only reason corporate entities and governments issue bonds is to raise money while stocks may also be issued to comply with government regulations. While the money raised during an IPO goes a long way to boost the company's operations, it is often held as liquid assets because an IPO is simply a matter of a business going public to increase its legitimacy and boost public confidence in its products. An initial public offering is a statement that a company is past the start-up stage. A bond issue means nothing more than that a company needs money for operations and wishes to borrow.

Another area where stocks and bonds differ is in maturity. While bonds come with a pre-arranged maturity date, stocks are perpetual. One can hold on to a stock for as long as they wish, collecting dividends on their investment for as long as a whole century. The longest maturity time for a bond is about 30–50 years.

The way that investors make money from either a stock or a bond also differs. With a stock, the price appreciates over time, raising the purported value of an investment (the money a person would make if they sold their shares at this exact moment). This rise is determined by the laws of demand and supply, such that when the market perceives the company as being healthy financially, the price rises because there is greater demand. The opposite is true when the company is struggling financially and enjoys no confidence in the stock market.

From an investment perspective, stocks and bonds differ in one key area, and that is the perception of security for them both. A stock is viewed as a volatile investment because its price is likely to drop at any time. Even though the overall interest rate of publicly traded companies maintains the lower double digits levels, some perform very badly and often go into the negative for protracted periods of time. This volatility makes it extremely hard to predict the return that an investment will bring. For a bond, the interest rate is predetermined and mostly fixed, save for slight deviations up and down, depending on the state of the economy and interest rates. A bond is considered to be safe and conservative, bringing a stabilizing effect to an investment portfolio. Stocks, on the other hand, come with high risk and high reward and tend to make a portfolio substantially more unpredictable.

Chapter 5 Day and Swing Trading

Now we are going to look at a short-term strategy used to earn cash in the here and now, rather than investing in companies for long term growth. These strategies take advantage of the short-term changes in the stock price in order to realize profits. The two methods we will discuss here are:

- Day Trading: When you day trade, you buy and sell the same security on the same trading day. This is a highly regulated activity. A brokerage will determine that you are a day trader if you execute 4-day trades within any 5-business day period (that makes you a "Pattern Day Trader"). To be a day trader, most brokerages require you to have $25,000 in your account. There are a few firms that will let you day trade with small accounts, but they charge large commissions. As a result, those companies are used by new day traders without much capital to learn, but experienced traders use regular brokerages so that they can avoid the high fees.
- Swing Trading: this is a lower risk strategy. This is simply a buy-low and sell-high strategy that can last any time length you want but up to a maximum of a few months. A swing trader doesn't day trade, so at a minimum, a swing trader will hold an investment overnight. Swing trading is a much lower risk unless the company

goes bankrupt or there is a huge recession (and hopefully you are doing your research so that you know what is possible) the stock is probably going to go higher than what you paid for it at some point in the near future. Since its lower risk, swing trading has no capital requirements.

Despite the differences, the techniques used are the same. Day trading is considered a high-risk activity, higher risk than swing trading, and much higher risk than normal stock investing. It's hard to say that swing trading is really that high risk as compared to buying shares of an individual stock for any purpose. If it's not profitable to sell, the swing trader can just hang on to the stock.

Goals and Risks

The goal of day traders and swing traders is to make cash profits. So, you can think of it as a *trading business* rather than acting as an investor. You are more concerned with the short-term fluctuations in stock price than you are with the long-term prospects of the company. For the day trader, they are looking at profiting off of price fluctuations that happen over the course of hours, minutes, and even seconds. A swing trader is looking to take advantage of price swings in the share price that occur over periods of days, weeks, or even several months.

One risk, especially with day trading, is that emotion will take hold. This can happen with positive and negative emotions. So, you might have too much fear of loss and get out too early, or you might get greedy and not sell when you should because you have dreams of the share price skyrocketing.

Another risk is new traders don't use standard methods of mitigating risk that can minimize loss of capital when your speculations go wrong. In the next section, we will discuss some techniques that can be used to help guard your account against massive losses. One problem is many people simply jump on and start trading without really knowing what is going on. Instead, you should take the time to invest in yourself and take some courses on day trading from professionals. A search online will reveal that there are many different courses available. Many come with stock market simulators that you can practice with the learn the art of day or swing trading.

Potential gains

Most new day traders will probably lose money, at least at first. However, if you've put the time in to study and done some practice, including taking a course, you might be on the way to becoming a successful day trader. Those that are successful can make high annual incomes.

Risk Mitigating Steps

Before we review the techniques used to evaluate moves on the stock market, let's look at some important risk-mitigating steps you must take in order to successfully day trade without losing all your capital.

Clear Sell Criteria

If you are looking to profit off the rise in a stock price, then have a specific target in mind and sell when it reaches the target. Let's say you buy shares of a given stock at $10 a share, and it starts rising. You set a profit target at $15 a share. When it hits that you sell it and book your profits, and you don't let emotion get the best of you and fret if it does up to $20 a share. A greedy trader or one who gets overly excited might hold the stock too long, hoping it will just keep rising. But then suddenly it might drop back down to even a lower level than what they paid for it. You should have a profit target in mind when you buy your shares and stick to it no matter what happens.

Stop Loss Order

A lot of new traders don't put in stop loss orders. Use the 1% rule (don't risk more than 1% of your total account value on one trade) to set the level for your stop loss order. What a stop loss order does, is it automatically puts a sell order for your shares if the price drops to a certain value or less. So, if you buy shares of stock at $16 a share, you can put a stop loss order at $15. Then if the stock price drops to $15, your shares are automatically sold, limiting your total loss to $1 a share. If it continues dropping to say $7 a share, you can see how you've saved yourself a huge amount of grief.

Putting a daily limit

You can also help protect yourself by putting a daily limit on the amount of capital you're willing to risk each day. So maybe you only allow yourself to buy $3,000 worth of shares (or whatever) so that you're not betting the farm.

Avoid trading on the margin

Using margin trading (borrowing money from the broker) is where a lot of people get themselves into financial trouble. If you don't spend what you don't have, then you can avoid getting in trouble in the first place. Instead of letting yourself get emotional about some supposedly "sure thing", have a steady plan for profits that you earn over the course of time, rather than hoping that you've "found the big thing" and you're going to possibly get yourself in huge trouble by borrowing a lot of money to realize your dreams, when the odds are solid your predictions will be wrong.

Calculating risk

Let's look at how advisors recommend you calculate your risk. The risk on a single trade should be 1% of the capital in your account. Let's say that shares of a given stock are trading at $100 and you have an account with $50,000. So, 1% of $50,000 is $500. That means the most you can risk is $500, but that doesn't apply to the total amount spent on buying the shares, so you don't buy $500 worth of shares. What it means is that you put a stop loss order to limit your total loss to $500. So, if you put a stop loss order at $99, that is a $1 loss per share, so you could buy 500 shares. So, you could risk your entire $50,0000 account on the trade! But with the stop loss, if the stock starts tanking, you'd automatically sell at $99 a share, so you'd have $49,500 at the end of the day. Suppose it dropped to $75 a share. With the stop-loss order, it would have no impact on you. But if you didn't have the stop loss order, you would have lost $12,500 on the trade.

Candles

When people day or swing trade, they use "technical analysis" in order to estimate future moves of the stock. The only difference between the two trading styles is the time frames over which the analysis is done. A day trader might be looking at 5-minute intervals to determine what trades to make over the next few hours, while a swing trader might be looking over the course of a few weeks for big swings in stock price.

One tool that is used in the analysis is candles. You can see candles on any stock chart by selecting them as a display option, and you can also set the time duration. Candles were actually invented by Japanese rice traders. Markets are universal.

The candles have "wicks" sticking out from them. These indicate the high and low prices for the time period. Candles are red or green in color. A red candle indicates selling off is dominant, while a green color indicates buying is dominant. Or put another way red candle is associated with dropping stock prices, and green candles are associated with rising stock prices.

The top wick is the high share price for the period. The bottom wick is the low share price for the period. what the period depends on is what you select for the chart options. So, if you are looking at the chart with 5-minute intervals, the high and low prices indicate the high and low prices for each 5-minute interval.

The body is the solid block. If the block is green, then the top of the body is the closing price (time at the end of the time interval), and the bottom of the body is the opening price (price at the start of the time interval). For a red candle, it's the opposite, so the top is the opening price, and the bottom is the closing price. So, a red candle indicates the price dropped for the given time period; a green candle indicates the price rose over the given time period.

Traders use candles to estimate changes in the direction of the stock price. If a candle of one color engulfs the previous candle of the other color, that is its body is much larger in size, that can indicate a price reversal is coming. You can see it in the picture above, there is a red candle with a small body next to a green candle with a very large body, and that large green candle was followed by an increase in the share price. The large green body indicates that over that time interval, a large number of people bought shares of the stock, and increased demand means prices will be bid upwards.

A hammer is a candlestick with a small body and a long wick below it.

A green hammer at the bottom of a downtrend can indicate that stock prices are about to go higher. So that is a buy signal. If the hammer is upside down, it's called an inverted hammer or a shooting star, for a red candlestick. These occur at the tops of uptrends, and that indicates the stock price is about to begin dropping. A shooting star is a sell signal.

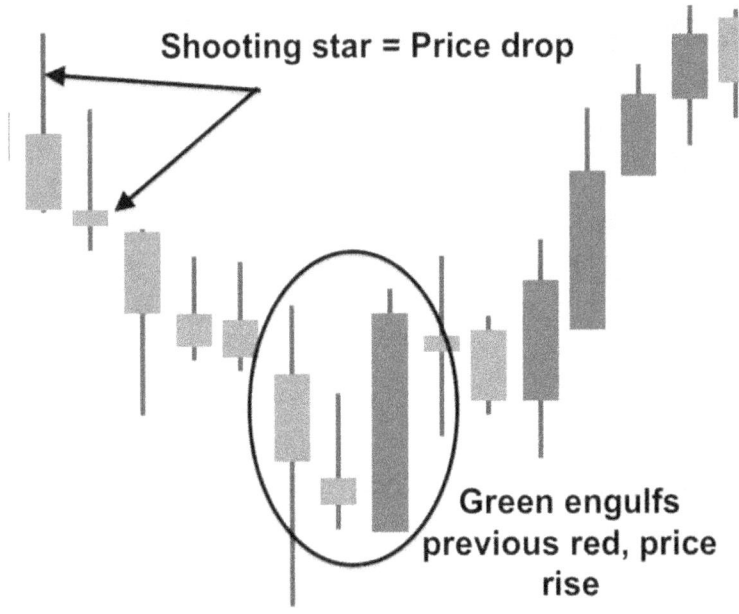

Moving Averages

Another tool that is used in the analysis by traders is looking at moving averages. You can set the number of days (periods) over which you want the stock chart to display the moving average. Moving averages reduce the noise normally found in stock charts so that you can view price trends as smooth curves. Traders often look at charts with two moving averages, one a short-term moving average and one a long-term moving average. When the two moving averages cross each other, then movements in the stock price are expected to follow. You can use either simple moving averages, which is just the average of stock prices over a given period, or an exponential moving average, which is more sensitive to recent changes in price.

Support and Resistance

Traders look for signs of support and resistance in stock charts. Support occurs at the bottom of stock prices, while resistance occurs at the top of stock prices. Support is a price level that defines the floor for a given stock. That is the price never seems to drop below that value. Resistance is the ceiling for a given stock. So that price of the stock doesn't rise above that value.

Bollinger Bands

Bollinger bands use the standard deviation for the stock price to set levels of support and resistance for the share price. The upper Bollinger band represents a high price level that the share price is unlikely to exceed. Remember that we are talking about short term time periods here, this is for day trading or swing trading. The lower Bollinger band represents a price below which the stock is unlikely to drop. The width of the bands also gives us an idea of how much variability there is in the stock price. Below is a chart of Amazon with Bollinger bands. It shows that for the past six months, the stock price could not get above $1966.21.

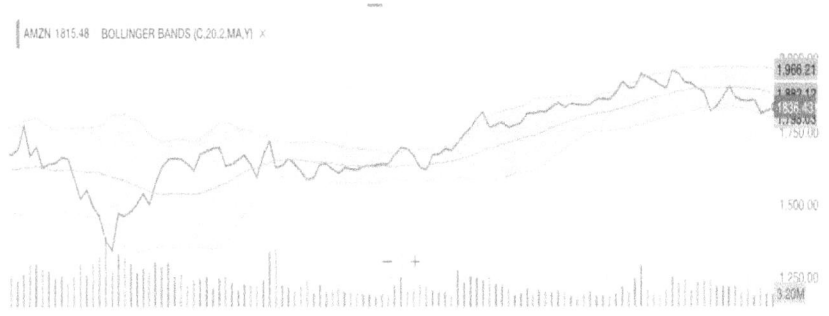

Bollinger bands are dynamic, so always change as the stock price moves. You can see how in recent months the bands for Amazon are much narrower, indicating that the price variability has dropped quite a bit, although if you look at the chart you'll note that the wide bands on the left are almost entirely due to the one decline in price that led up to Christmas eve 2018.

Summary

Day trading and swing trading are not for everyone, but they can be used to generate short term profits. Some people like the analysis and getting involved in the short term moves of the stock, so taking a very active role in trading. If the idea intrigues you but day trading seems too risky, consider swing trading, which really isn't that risky in comparison, but you should always use stop-loss orders and be ready to take profits when they come rather than holding too long hoping to get more profits. Also, it's possible to mix things up, and you can put some of your capital into long term investments and use other capital to fund some level of swing or day trading. As we will see later, people interested in short term profits in the stock market can also use options trading.

Chapter 6 Forex Trading

The foreign exchange currency market, more commonly written as the forex market, is the largest of all the investment markets, currently boasting more than $4 trillion dollars' worth of transactions per day, or roughly 10 times more than what the New York Stock Exchange can manage. Despite the lucrative potential available in this market, it was long outside the realm of the amateur trader as technological limitations made it difficult to amass the information required for such an undertaking. Luckily, the rise of the internet, along with countless online forex trading platforms, means that anyone who is interested can take advantage of the extreme leverage rates available in the market to turn a small initial investment into a serious payday.

Before jumping in with both feet, you are going to want to keep in mind the fact that the forex market is completely speculative which means that unlike in most markets when you buy and sell in the forex market you aren't actually gaining anything physical in the process. Unlike the stock market where you acquire shares in a specific company, for example, in the forex market, all you are doing is moving numbers around in various computer databases with relevant information relating to the countries in question causing them to either move in one direction or another. Your gains and losses are then expressed in the currency of your choosing.

If this seems like a bit of an odd system, that's because the forex market only exists because international organizations and countries needed an easy way to move currency around in massive quantities without going through the steps the average person would be required to do such a thing. These entities tend to trade in units of currency that are so extreme they can actually affect the overall value of the currencies being traded, which is where the speculative side of the market comes into play.

Generally speaking, only about 20 percent of the movement in the forex market is from these major entities, with the rest coming from investors that are trying to make a buck from the movement that spreads out through the market as a result. While a majority of these investors are professionals working for financial institutions or hedge funds, more and more private traders are jumping on the bandwagon each year, drawn to the promise of potentially huge wins thanks to the available leverage.

Forex facts

The most important thing to keep in mind when trading in the forex market is that each forex trade is actually a pair of disparate trades because you are always selling one currency in order to pay for another. Forex trades are made in three separate sizes, known as lots. A micro lot is 1,000 units of a given currency while a mini lot is 10,000 units of a currency and a standard lot is 100,000 units of a specific currency.

When the market moves, the smallest amount that is tracked is known as a pip which is one percent of the total price of the currency in question. When you are first starting out in the forex market you are going to want to avoid taking on trades that are larger than a micro lot as in this case the pip is worth 10 cents of the currency you are working with. This means you won't quickly lose your shirt when a trade turns against you in the last moment. If you stray to mini lots or standard lots you run the risk of losing $1 or $10 respectively, per pip. For reference, you can expect a trending currency to move around 100 pips per trading session.

While the forex market differs from other markets in key ways, it is important to always keep in mind that it is the same in the ways that matter the most as it is driven by supply and demand as much as any other market. This means that when a certain currency is in high demand then the value of that currency will naturally continue to increase until the point where the market has more sellers than it does buyers, at which point the price will start to drop until the buyers start to bite once more.

When trading in the forex market it is extremely important to be aware of instances where a specific currency is about to increase in demand so that you can jump on it as quickly as possible.

This means you will want to keep abreast of things like economic predictions related to world powers, current geopolitical strife and key interest rate movements. It is important to keep in mind there is no such thing as insider trading when it comes to the forex market, as such anything you learn about is fair game.

Another important fact to keep in mind is that the forex market never closes from Monday to Friday, it just shifts its focus. While closed on the weekends, during the week the market naturally shifts its focus between various currency pairs based on the portion of the world that is currently the most active. For example, the currency pair USD/JPY would be active during the portion of the day when the US is active and again when Japan is active. The forex market is divided into three segments based on the time of day in the US, Asia and Europe. This isn't anything that is strictly regulated, as the forex market isn't regulated in any traditional sense, rather it is simply more profitable to trade a specific currency when it is the most active.

While you can likely find someone willing to buy or sell into any currency pair imaginable, there are 18 primary currency pairs that are traded most of the time. These pairs are made up of only eight different currencies which means you should aim to be familiar with each of them if you want to find any success in the market in the long-term. These are AUD the Australian dollar, CAD the Canadian dollar, CHF the Swiss franc, EUR the euro, GBP the British pound, JPY the Japanese yen, NZD the New Zealand dollar and USD the US dollar. Knowing the currencies you can safely ignore early on is crucial to making your early forays into the market as successful as possible. There will always be time to mix things up at a later date after you have mastered the basics.

Lack of traditional regulation

As already noted, the forex market is not regulated in nearly the same way as other markets and is, in fact, considered an unregulated exchange. This essentially means that when someone chooses to make a trade dishonestly they are not going to be at the mercy of any regulatory body which means it is up to the community to dish out justice. As such, every trade in the forex market is based on what is known as a credit agreement which essentially means everyone operates in good faith. As anyone who breaks the agreement will never be able to trade in the forex market again, it tends to work fairly well in most instances.

In addition to this system, the US also has what's known as the National Futures Association which is a voluntary organization that forex dealers can join which holds its members to a higher standard than the market as a whole. It also offers arbitration options if a disagreement does occur. This means that when you are dealing with a Forex broker or dealer in the US then you are certainly going to want to ensure they are an NFA member.

As there is no one to enforce such things, the rules are more relaxed in the forex market as well. This means you are free to short sell as much currency as you have access to as long as you think you can make a profit off of it. On the other hand, there is also no limit to how many lots you can buy in a single trade which means you could make a billion dollar trade if you had the cash.

Finally, the number of traditional forex brokers are few and far between which means that a majority of forex transactions don't require a commission fee. Rather, forex dealers make their money off of the spread which means it is likely going to be a bit larger than what you may be used to. This means the forex market is principal only which means the dealers are taking on just as much risk as the traders. As such, it is impossible to buy on the bid or sell at the offer when trading in forex; however, this limitation is mitigated thanks to the fact that it can be much easier to make a profit when trading in the forex market as commission and fees don't come into account.

Currency trading facts

When trading in the currency market, the currency you are selling is a short position and the currency you are buying is a long position. As an example, if you make a trade of EUR/USD then you are going long on dollars while going short on euros which means you are selling euros and buying dollars.

As noted above, you really only need to focus on a handful of currencies in order to get a full understanding of the basics of forex trading.

As such, when you are taking your very first steps into the market then you will want to focus on USD/CHF, GDP/USD, USD/JPY and EUR/USD. In addition to these pair, you will want to keep an eye out for the commodity pairs, so named because the related countries tend to move commodities around in large amounts. These include NZD/USD, USD/CAD and AUD/USD. Finally, with the addition of EUR/GBP, GBP/JPY, and EUR/JPY, you have more than 90 percent of the trades made on the average day covered.

Reading a currency quote

Regardless of the currencies, you are working with, they will all be quoted in a specific way. The first half of the currency pair is referred to as the base currency while the second is referred to as either the counter currency or the base currency. As a general rule USD is the default base currency and gains tend to be written in dollars per the other currency and when they are quoted will include both an ask price and a bid price.

The bid price is the amount the forex dealer will ultimately be willing to purchase the base currency for, and it will be written in an amount of the secondary currency. Alternately, the ask price is the amount that a dealer can expect to sell any base currency for and is typically written in the counter currency. The difference between the bid price and the ask price is where the spread comes from and is typically written out to the fourth decimal place.

Don't forget margin and rollover

In order to trade in the forex market successfully in the long-term, you will need to take margin into account in a different way than you would with other markets. Specifically, in the forex market, your margin ceases to be a down payment on potential future equity and is instead best thought of as an account deposit that can be accurately used to help mitigate losses related to forex trades that may go south down the line. Generally speaking, the greater the leverage a dealer allows, the greater the margin on the trade is likely to be.

When it comes to completing a required forex trade, the general rule is you must complete your side of the trade within 48 hours. This period of time can be extended, however, through the use of a rollover which pushes the due date back a full 48 hours in addition for a percentage of interest paid on the transaction. A rollover can be used multiple times, though the fees are cumulative so it is important to track them closely for the best results. Rollovers are also trade in the forex market just like currencies.

When taking advantage of a rollover transaction, it is important to keep in mind that the difference between the interest rate of the base currency and the counter currency can be properly visualized via an overnight loan. When utilizing this type of loan, a trader will hold onto the long position of a currency based on the assumption that it has a greater interest rate to gain an advantage from.

The amount gained from the rollover will then vary day to day depending on the interest rate's variance. If this all sounds too complicated, avoiding a rollover is easy, all you have to do is avoid holding any positions overnight.

Leverage

When trading in the forex market you can think of leverage as money that is being borrowed expressly for the purpose of potential increasing returns should a given trade go according to plan. While not advisable for those who are first getting into the forex market, you can easily find rates of greater than 100 to 1 which means it is possible to gain the benefits of trading a lot while only having the cash on hand to pay for a micro lot. It is important to remember, however, that if things don't go according to plan then you are going to be on the hook for a lot's worth of loss so trade carefully.

As such, it can be effective to think of leverage as magnifying the movement of the market as a whole. Some of the losses that you could potentially experience when using leverage can be mitigated through a fastidious use of stop losses or through the use of a margin watcher. A margin watcher is a type of software program that comes with a variety of online trading platforms and allows users to set parameters to ensure that their losses are never going to be any greater than they absolutely have to be.

Tools of the trade

The truth of the matter is that a trader is only ever as good as their tools. Taking the time to ensure that you have the right tools before you start trading is one of the most reliable ways to improve your results and ensure that your trading capital balance moves in the way you want it to. What follows are a list of the most important tools you should make sure to have in your pocket before you get serious about forex trading.

Trading journal: The first tool that every forex trader needs might surprise you as it is neither high tech nor expensive. Rather, it is recommended that you get a pen and a notebook and keep track of every trade you make religiously. You will want to write down every pair you identify as promising and write down the results of every trade you make. What's more, doing this in a physical notebook is recommended as opposed to an online alternative because the physical act of writing everything down will give you more time to focus on the trades you've made, making it easier to gather insight that you might miss if you are just imputing numbers on a screen or, even worse, having them automatically tracked for you. The fact of the matter is that writing things down for yourself actually improves memory retention when compared to either hearing or seeing them. This goes the same for typing as well, nothing beats the good old-fashioned approach.

When keeping track of your trades you are going to want to include the time of day and the date the trade took place, what you set your stop-losses at, your entry and exit points, the reasons you decided to make the trade and the results. You are also going to want to make note if any emotions influenced your decision or any other extraneous variables that came into play. Keeping track of your trades in this fashion will help to make it easier for you to see what your trends are, how your trading plan is performing and where your weaknesses are coming from, ideally so you can correct them before they cost you any more money.

Broker: A good broker can easily make the difference between completing a trade successfully and watching as the right moment to strike passes you by. Unfortunately finding the right one can be easier said than done, simply because the market is so crowded with options. The first thing you are going to need to consider when choosing a broker is their relative level of security. You are going to want to find a broker that is in your own country, or at least that is in a country that provides oversight for these types of transactions. If you fail to do so your money could potentially disappear and you could have no recourse when it comes to getting it back. If you are in the US you are going to want to ensure that the broker you chose is a member of the CFTC and is also registered with the NFA. Additionally, you are going to want to ensure that they have a reliable track record and have been in business for at least 5 years.

You are also going to need to consider the amount required for an initial deposit and ensure it is in line with what you are willing to spend in order to start trading in the forex market successfully. While finding the brokers with the lowest required minimums is a common practice, it is also important to consider that those brokers might not be as stalwart when it comes to services as those who have a higher minimum. A required balance of around $500 should ensure that you are getting the right mix of budgetary concerns and reliability.

It is also important to consider the spread that the broker works from as this can vary dramatically and if you don't look into it you can easily be taken advantage of. Policies regarding withdrawals and fees for deposits will also vary and it is important to ensure that you are comfortable with all of these policies before you commit to a specific broker. You will also need to keep in mind margin requirements and leverage ratios, generally the lower the better if you are a new trader. Greater levels of leverage are useful for those who are more experienced but while you are starting out trading with your own money is encouraged.

Quality charting software: While the online platform of the broker you choose is likely going to offer some charting options, in order to trade in forex successfully you are most likely want to go above and beyond the standard and seek out other charting software as well, especially if you are interested in technical analysis. The right tools for you are going to vary based on the strategies you plan on employing which means you are going to want to work out your initial trading plan and the strategies that appeal to you before looking into alternatives in this space.

Economic calendar: The forex market is known to be extremely volatile which, depending on who you ask, is part of its charm. There are certain periods of time where it is going to be much more volatile than others, however, which is why having a reliable economic calendar is so important. Much of this volatility comes from fundamental announcements, most of which are scheduled ahead of time. These are major events that help shed light on the economic standing of a company which means you really don't want to miss them which is where the calendar comes into play. A good calendar will update for these events automatically so that you don't need to go looking for the dates instead. Many programs available these days offer apps as well as software that work in tandem so you can keep track of important information even when you are on the go.

Time zone convertor: As you know, the forex market is open 24/5 which means it will often behoove you to know what time it is in the other major markets. This means that the best time to trading is often when two major time zones overlap as you get the benefit of double volatility in many instances. A good time zone convertor will allow you to see which market is active when so that you don't miss out.

Volatility calculator: The name volatility calculator is actually a bit misleading as it is more of a tracker of what volatilities certain currencies have had at certain points in time. This will let you track past performance as a way of anticipating future results. Using this regularly will help to ensure you are always getting the most bang for your trading buck.

Forex lingo to know

Cable, sterling, pound: These are the various names that you will see the UK's currency referenced as.

Greenback, buck: These are the most common slang terms for the US dollar in forex circles.

Swissie: You will often see the Swiss franc referred to as a Swissie in forex media.

Aussie: You will often see the Australian dollar referred to as the Aussie in forex publications.

Kiwi: You will often see the New Zealand dollar referred to as the Kiwi in forex publications.

Loonie, Little Dollar: You will often see the Canadian dollar referred to as the Little Dollar or sometimes the Loonie in forex publications.

Yard: A billion units of a specific currency is referred to as a yard

Chapter 7 Options Trading

Traditional day trading strategies did not include the use of options. Things have changed now and most people are making reasonable profits in trading options.

This book highlights some of the advantages and disadvantages of options trading and provides you with relevant information on the types of options. You will also learn how to set up a trade and get a few tips on how to become an expert in the business of trading options.

Examples of Top Brokers Trading Options

Before we begin, let us look at some of the top brokers that major in trading options.

1. Plus500

The Plus500 online CFD and Forex trading platform is a leading brand when it comes to trading options. It offers trading facilities on commodities, Forex, indices, and options via the Webtrader platform.

2. AvaTrade

This is one of the pioneers in online trading, and a leading CFD and Forex broker since 2006. Since its establishment, AvaTrade has remained to be one of the main traders of over 250 instruments, including commodities, stocks, indices, and options.

The platform has hundreds of thousands of users who carry out over 2 million trades within one month.

3. IG

IG is also a leading provider of Forex, cryptocurrencies, options and indices across several thousands of markets. This award-winning platform is regulated by the FCA and has a track record of excellence that spans over 40 years.

4. *Interactive Broker*

Interactive Broker is one of the most reliable and big Broker out there, it offers basically all the financial products worldwide. If you decide to use options as a day trader, you want to watch an important factor which is the commission plan. IB is one of the cheapest broker in regard to commissions and of course.

Options Definition

By definition, an option is a financial derivative or contract that allows you to purchase or sell a financial asset within a predetermined cost and time frame. The predetermined date or time frame is also known as the exercise date. For options trading to take place, the seller must meet all the requirements of the trade.

Options trading differs from market to market, and from platform to platform. As a trader, you must be able to differentiate between the various categories of options, including ETF options, stock options, and futures options among several others.

Options are considered a low-risk form of trade because you can terminate a contract before the exercise or expiry date. The value of an option only represents a percentage of a seller's underlying security or asset.

The price at which the buyer agrees to place for the option is called the strike price while the fee used to purchase the option contract is called the premium.

What is an Option Contract?

An option contract is basically an agreement struck connecting two traders to trade an asset at an established date and price. Option contracts are common in the trade of commodities, securities as well as real estate investments.

Normally, an option contract comprises of the following:

1. The type of Option - This can either be a call or put option. A call option allows you to purchase a specific number of shares over time while a put option is for buying shares of a certain commodity or security on specified terms.
2. The Unit of Trade refers to a single indivisible amount of any trade item. For options, the common unit of trade is a contract.
3. The Strike Price – as stated earlier, this is the price at which an options contract can be exercised (sold or bought). In the case of a call option, it is the cost where the shares are

bought by the buyer before the expiration date. For the put option, it refers to the cost at which the shares can be sold by the buyer before the expiration date.
4. Underlying security is the commodity, bond, index, currency or stock used to establish the worth of an option. This value is derived from the price or performance of the underlying security.
5. Expiration Date is the last day for buying or selling an option.

Other Types of Options

Besides the call and put options, there are several other types of options you can trade in on the market. These are categorized using the methods used for trade, underlying securities, and the expiration cycle. You, however, have to bear in mind that not all of them are suitable for intraday trading. Some of these options include:

- Index options
- Options on futures
- Stock options
- Weekly SPY options
- Mini and Mini Index options
- ETF options
- IRA Accounts
- QQQ options
- Crude oil options
- OEX options
- ES Weekly options

- ITM options
- E-Mini options
- S & P options

The Underlying Asset

Although most options are derived from shares in listed companies such as Amazon and Twitter, a good number of them are from alternative underlying securities such as real estate investment trusts, stock indexes, commodities, and currencies.

Stock Options

Before engaging yourself in trading stock options, it is important to understand that contracts will be defined by the underlying stock. In most cases, this will be 100 shares of the stock although it may change due to changes in stock mergers and splits.

Regional Differences

Options trading is mostly done in America. One advantage of American options is that you can buy or sell the options at any time between the purchase date and the expiration date. European options are least traded because you can only exercise them at the end of the contract period.

Options and Futures

Most people who have traded in futures can easily realize the similarity with options. Both make use of contracts and work using the same underlying instrument. However, there exists a difference in the trading procedure and rules. Trading in options gives you a wider variety of options that can be traded separately or in combination with stock trades for insurance purposes. A future contract's value is often very different from an option's value. While the worth of futures is tied to the value of the underlying security and delivery dates, the cost of an option depends on the time premium as well as the value of the contract.

In terms of the profit and loss potential, the amount of money a trader can gain or lose in a futures contract is often very large compared to options trading. Execution of a futures contract depends on a predetermined date, often stated in the. An options contract can be closed at any time depending on the performance of the trade.

Why You Should Trade Options

Let us look at some of the most notable reasons why one may need to trade options, besides making serious money.

Low prices – while trading options, you can create and close contracts faster and with minimal risk compared to other securities. The cost of purchasing an option is relatively cheaper than that of buying the underlying security, or shares in the case of stock trading. This means that you can make more profit using less capital.

High possibility of success – it is easier to make a profit from options since you do not need to close a contract to gain from it. Options are also highly volatile.

Diverse markets – there are numerous investment opportunities related to options trading. These opportunities are often cheaper than the purchase of actual stock. The more you increase your capital, the more your profit potential grows.

It can be combined with stock trade – to maximize profits, you can easily combine options with stock trading. Doing this allows you to increase your stock from the profits made in trading options.

Easy to access – various online platforms give you the opportunity to trade options from all over the world. With some good capital, all you need is a good internet connection to get started.

Disadvantages

Despite the many benefits of options trading, there are a few drawbacks that come with it. However, these are less likely to impact your experience in the trade and can be overlooked. Some disadvantages that come to mind include:

An extensive spread – a bid-ask spread is a variation between the maximum price that the buyer is ready to place and the minimum price the seller is prepared to allow for the asset. The spread is quite wide when selling options as compared to stocks trade. This is due to the reduced liquidity associated with the options markets and has a great impact on the profit of any daily trade.

Reduced price movements – in trading options, the changes in the price is limited to the time value of the contract and premium. Although this value increases with the cost of the underlying instrument, the profit may be reduced significantly in case the time value diminishes.

These drawbacks are highly insignificant and should not prevent you from engaging in the trade of options. You can easily adjust your trading plans to minimize their impact.

How to Start Trading Options

Trading options is straightforward. Beginners can join the team of traders in a few steps as highlighted below:

1. Create a Brokerage Account

You need this account to easily liaise with your traders. Since options trading has become so much popular, the internet has a good number of brokers to select from. You must, however, ensure that you get one that suits your trading needs. When selecting an online broker, put the following factors into consideration.

- The account type – first you need to determine if you need a margin or cash account. The latter account only allows you to trade the capital in your possession while the former account gives you the chance to borrow capital from your brokers. A margin account gives you a better standing in terms of profits since it also allows you to sell options without necessarily having an underlying asset.

- The cost - carry out some research on different brokers and compare their charges in terms of commission. This will ensure that you get the best competitive spreads. Be sure to check out whether there are hidden charges as well.
- The trading platform – you must understand that you will be spending a good amount of time on the platform. It is therefore important that you get one with the essential technical tools and charts for your trade. If you intend to trade as you move around, be sure to check whether the mobile and tablet version of the platform exists.

2. Develop a Strategy

Once you are done creating a brokerage account, you will need to create a winning strategy. Options trading strategies come in various designs. Some are straightforward while others need a lot of time and resources. A good strategy is one that has several components in it. These include

- *Charts and patterns*

Charts and patterns are a must for each trading engagement. They help you study and easily understand the history of an option. Each chart must have a good indicator for trading options. These indicators vary for each strategy and may include the Money Flow Index, Relative Strength Index, Bollinger Bands, Open Interest, and the Put-Call Ratio Indicator. You need more time to understand and practice pattern trading with options. However, you will need to try out a number of charts until you get one that is straightforward and easy to understand.

Timing

When it comes to trading options, time is of the essence. You must understand when to set up a trade, enter into contracts and when to make an exit. For a strategy to work there must be a trader who is willing to place contracts early enough. For instance, you may need to start as early as 6:00 am if you want to get the direction of the day's trade early enough.

Once you have determined the day's trend, you can use the information to come up with a strategy depending on how the market has been at night. You can take the E-mini option for example since up to 70% of stocks are entitled to move in the same direction during the day. It is good to note that the US stock market dictates the direction of trade in other countries. So, it is important to give the market an hour every morning for it to stabilize before sealing any contracts for the day

Intraday traders need a lot of time and a careful investigation of the market. Make an adequate analysis of the market in case you want to make considerable profits.

Example

One basic strategy that works is buying calls or selling puts when the market is rising. Wait until the market is deteriorating for you to buy puts or sell calls. Most people do sell options more than they buy. If you land on an equity that is quite predictable, you may buy an option to yield more profit then wait for it to start declining to make a sale. One example of such equity is Apple.

Chapter 8 How to Create Passive Income with Dividend Stocks

Passive income refers to the type of income that you create even when sleeping: it is something desired by many. This income generation method can build your wealth either by helping cover your monthly expenses or reinvesting. Dividends are the best fit as a passive income source. This is because the income is sustainable, requires little maintenance, grows faster than inflation and can also be tax-advantaged. It might take you time to get a reasonable amount of dividend income, but time is always on your side in this case.

What Are Dividends?

Dividends, just like many other financial subjects, are simple at on the surface but very complicated underneath. From a surface point of view, dividends are paid to give out a company's earnings to its shareholders. You must be aware that being a shareholder in a company that pays dividends `entitles you a share of its profits. A perfect dividend policy is beneficial to both the company and the shareholder. Many investors chose to invest in great dividend-paying companies as the basis of their portfolio. This technique is referred to as dividend growth investing.

In this case, growth refers to the growth of dividend payments over some time. Since the 1990s, the average annual dividend increase is always around 6%. This, however, is not a fixed rate; it isn't unheard of for companies to have a yearly dividend of 10% or more!

Dividend Investing

If you are not sure about dividend investing is, this topic is for you. As mentioned earlier, dividends refer to a way companies share success with its shareholders. It is like a portion of the total earnings paid out you as the shareholder. You can choose to get your dividends in the form of cash or more shares. You might want to know what dividend dates are? For instance, a company can declare a dividend of Y dollars. The day this information was relayed is known as the declaration date, the time is, however not that important. When looking at a dividend, there are two significant dates you should know. Ex-Dividend Date- you must own a stock before this date so that you can receive the bonus. Payment Date- This is the day money is paid to shareholders. The Record Date is technically the date you need to be recorded as a shareholder to be entitled to dividends. This date is always two business days after the ex-dividend date: this is solely because trades take two days to settle. It has lesser importance to an investor than the ex-dividend date. It is, however, good to know what the record date is. Additionally, pay more attention to the ex-dividend date!

How to Compare Stocks for Dividend Investing

There are two ways you can look at dividends and determine how good they are. Both of them are pure math. The dividend yield is a certain percentage showing the amount of money the profit is compared to the share price. The higher the amount, the better: this means you earn more passive income out of your investment. For example, if the average dividend amount of the company is 3.46%, it means you earned $3.45 in dividends for every $100 you invested. The second you can use to determine whether the dividend id proper is the dividend payout ratio: this refers to the paid dividends and divided by the company's total earnings. You should ask yourself if the company make sufficient profit to the cover for the dividends they promised you.

Lastly, look at the dividend growth rate. Most companies tend to increase their dividends over time, and this metric establishes the rate at which they do so. The higher your dividend payment grows, the more your passive income grows. If you remember, we said earlier that the average dividend growth rate for most companies is around 6%. Put in mind that you are building a 6-figure portfolio that may contain individual stocks or various funds. And, don't just look at the dividend! It is only a smaller part of the bigger picture in this case. Instead, look at the stocks and the company growth rate as a whole

When to Reinvest or Not to Reinvest

Remember, when we discussed the two options when it comes to when acquiring your dividend? You should consider that in this situation. It can be easier two chose to base on that because you will know what your investment objectives are. Here, the simple thing you ought to do is taking the dividend in cash form. You now have the cash you can do whatever you want with. If you prefer passive income to withdraw the money from your trading account, this is the option you should go with.

Considering your age, this could be the best decision as you will take advantage of the compounding magic. On the other hand, reinvesting your dividends enables your shares to compound into more shares. Companies make it easy to do this through a feature called The Dividend Re-Investment Plan (DRIP). DRIP automatically converts all your dividends paid into the shares without charging you a commission, and in some cases, you will get a 2-3% discount. To enroll in the DRIP program, simply consult your stockbroker. For your information, not even stock has a DRIP; its existence depends on the company's management decision.

Dividend Growth Investing: Case Study

In this case, we make up a situation to show you just how great dividend growth investing can be. Let us assume you bought $10,000 worth of Toyota shares on the New York Stock Exchange in early 1999. Below is how much you will have at the moment. 243 share of Toyota worth $41.02 each $4296.34 in passive income in the next 12 months ($1.22 per share annually) 2.96% dividend yield ($296.45/$10,000). You should note that the example had to be set in the USA Stock Exchange because all these financial calculators online-only support American tickers. Fast forward to 2019; you made five times your initial investment mainly due to capital gains. Interestingly, your passive income grew even more, multiplying itself more than seven times the initial amount. The outcome (passive income growth) was due to two factors: dividend reinvestments and dividend pay raise.

How to Start Chasing Dividend Income

Below are the three steps you can take to start chasing your dividend income.

1. Pick a Type of Account

The first thing you need to do is pick a type of account you prefer to work with. Dividends are taxable in some countries, meaning you could benefit from keeping them legally registered accounts like RRSP or TFSA. Deciding where to place your investments can be a very confusing thing. Below is what you need to take away from this subtopic. TFSA: applies Canadian, American, and other international stocks and ETFs RRSP: Refers to Canadian, American, and other foreign stocks and ETFs. Unregistered Accounts: Canadian,

American, and other International stocks and any margin trading engagements (paying maximum taxes on dividends and handle riskier investments to get capital investments just in case an investment goes wrong). Generally, the fee charged on profits is lower than that charged on a regular income. There are, however, many rules and exceptions, especially regarding US Stocks. It is hard to find a one-fits-all answer, and I would recommend you to consult a professional, especially when your portfolio grows bigger.

2. Choose a Stockbroker

As you might know, the broker needs to provide the type of account you required in Step 1. You will also want a broker that offers a DRIP when chasing dividends. You should, therefore, be careful with the kind of broker you are opting for. Preferably, go for brokers that support registered accounts like RRSPs and TFSAs.

3. Decide between ETFs and Stocks

The essential dividend growth investing pertains to picking individual stocks using the metrics we discussed earlier in this article. There are plenty of ETFs in different countries that mainly focus on dividend income and have little management expenses. While ETFs charge a fee that digs into the returns, it is a shallow maintenance strategy. You don't need to look at individual companies and their payout ratios. Instead, what you need to focus on is the distribution you earn and the yield it provides you.

4. Keep on Contributing and Investing

This is a continuous process that does not stop once you purchase your first stocks. The case study we used above focused only on a one-time investment tracked over 20 years later. You should, therefore, be making regular deposits and slowly be picking up even more ETFs and dividend stocks. This will result in your passive income stream growing even at a faster rate. Ideally, you can use a DRIP where possible for most of your investment life to accelerate growth.

Creating Passive Income with Dividend Stocks

Dividends are passive income. You get the benefits of dividend income after investing some upfront time to make your decision. Additionally, you are a minority owner in the business and have no control in the decision-making process. Neither, do you have to spend much of your time managing your investments: just a few efficient readings and you are good to go. You can, therefore, carve out a little amount of time to keep an eye on your investments. With the increase in the speed of information and different mobile apps, the dividend has been made very easy in today's word. Historically, dividend investing has been regarded as a risk-averse method for investors to invest in the stock market.

Dividend investing is one of the best ways to increase income through passive income. Living off the bonuses is not a sprint but a marathon. You should not, however, take the marathon lightly. You should have the urge to increase both your income and your retirements. Plant your precious dividend seed by investing in the dividend growth stocks. What will it need? Well, an average dividend yield of around 3% in your portfolio, you will need approximately a $3.33 Million portfolio to earn $100,000 annually in dividend income.

The annual dividend yield refers to the calculation of the general percentage of a dividend per share in received in relation to the stock price. It is a good barometer of the annual income earned from investing in a stock. For example, if you invest in a $100 stock, and it pays $2 per share in dividends. This is equal to a 4% dividend yield a year.

It is not possible to start living off your dividends right away after investing, but it can happen over some time. But with a good plan and strategy, you can achieve the goal of passive income and living off dividends sooner than you imagine. The key to living off dividends is focusing on dividend growth stocks. The dividend growth stocks increase annually, which increases your income without you doing a single thing! Remember when I talked about planting a seed? Well, if you invest the right way, your seed will grow into a huge redwood tree!

How to Generate a Passive Income Annually from Dividend Stocks

So, how do you generate a passive income each year from dividend stocks? When you are building a dividend portfolio, start scaling smaller positions that you will continue to develop over sometime. First, use a brokerage that gives the lowest commission fee on trading. They are brokers that allow you to trade utterly commission-free on all the stocks and options. This is a very lucrative deal because options are usually essential to purchase. When properly used, options are an excellent way to mitigate risk in your account or portfolio. These are the best stocks when it comes to covered call writing.

As I have said many times before, investing in dividend stocks is the best way of generating passive income in the long run. However, choosing which stocks to involve in a dividend portfolio can be a challenging task for some investors. With the availability of a wide range of options, it could be very beneficial if you become selective and go beyond a company's dividend yield in search of the best opportunities. By so doing, it could lead to a more sustainable and higher passive income in the long run. Below are some of the aspects you should consider when it comes to investing in dividends.

Track Record

While the past performances might not be the best guide to the future, companies that have the unquestionable capability of delivering profits over a long period may be economic moats. For instance, they may have a stronger brand and lower costs. This suggests that their future dividend growth will be robust and resilient. This can be better if that company has a history of rewarding its shareholders by paying out dividends with profit gains.

Management Focus

Through reading and analyzing a company's annual report, you can be able to ascertain management standpoints in the future dividend growth. For instance, several management teams will pay attention to the reinvestment of excess capital to enhance future sales and the profitability of the business. As much as this can be a good move in some situations, it may not offer the most appealing outlook for investors seeking a passive income. Company management may apply a higher risk approach that looks to expand the business into new territories markets at a fast rate. This could imply that reduced dividend growth is just ahead. It could, therefore, be a good idea ensuring that the focus of company management from a risk/reward point of view, are aligned to those of the investor.

Company Type

While different industries like technology might offer more earnings growth ratio, they are doubtful to give generous dividend growth due to massive investments of capital. Similarly, a less mature business may need more significant investments and might be unable to pay out dividends to the shareholders. Therefore, it can be prudent for an investor to carefully assess the maturity of the business as well as its sector stability before purchasing. For the investors seeking more than just a passive income, mature stocks working in more established industries could be the right place to start when choosing the best income opportunities.

Diversification

As much as a lot of investors prefer to majorly focus on the potential return from investing their funds in the stock market, learning how to reduce the risk could be the most sensible starting point. After all, you can gain from getting a passive income in a short period, only for the dividend income to be hit by huge losses further down the line. Therefore, looking to reduce a company risk could be a worthy move. This is the danger posed by difficulties encountered by businesses that can lead to a decline in the stock price. In portfolios that have a small number of stocks, the company-specific risk will be extremely high due to a single stock's decline resulting in major loses for the general collection.

However, a well-diversified portfolio may not be impacted too severely even when one of its members experiences financial difficulties. While the general stock market provides the potential to make high levels of capital growth in the long run, it also allows creating a high rising passive income. As you might be aware, investing in any stock means you are risking. There will always be loopholes or chances of losing money should a business establishment fail to deliver as expected. You can, however, reduce the risk through diversification. Obtaining high yields may also help make the reward/risk ratio from the buying dividend stocks very appealing.

Additionally, holding income shares over a long period may keep costs to a minimum while earning an increasing passive income. In portfolios that have a small number of stocks, the company-specific risk will be extremely high due to a single stock's decline resulting in major loses for the general collection.

High Yields

As much as it might sound obvious that buying high-yield stocks is an excellent means of making a monthly passive income, it is nevertheless the quickest method of achieving that goal. When determining which stocks the investor might be interested in, it could be worth working in reverse. What this means is, first find out how much income you need in a single month. Secondly, consider the average yield you need from your portfolio to hit the target. This way, you will be in a better position to exclude those stocks that give dividend returns way too low to provide your preferred level of monthly income.

Long-Term hold

With the increasing number of stocks available to investors in different sectors and countries, it is very tempting to keep switching from one capital to the other depending on the current state of things in the economy. In terms of being the best way to use your funds, this may seem like the best idea at the time, but the harsh truth is that buying and selling regularly can result in inflated dealing costs. Similarly, it may also mean that stocks kept in a portfolio are not given the time they need to be profitable. Therefore, holding dividend stocks over a prolonged period of time could be the best method of generating a passive income. This means the investor will only use little effort and stand a good chance of potentially higher returns.

Assessing a company's record of growth and the way it pays its dividends, as well as its strategy, can lead to an increased growth rate in an investor's passive income. Similarly, assessing a company's maturity and the industry it's operating in may lead to more clear income outlook. Diversifying among a wide range of stocks can help cut risks while opting for stocks that match with the investor's risk/reward goals can lead to a better shareholder experience.

Chapter 9 Fundamentals of Investing in the Stock Market

Let's kick things off by discussing some theory pertaining to the stock market.

You hear references to the "stock market" all the time. You read about it in the news, and you certainly hear people talking about it at work, the bank, the grocery store, or at the park. It is everywhere. Yet, very few people seem to understand what it really means.

The stock market is just one type of market within the broader umbrella term known of "financial markets." As such, it is important to get a firm understanding of what financial markets are and where we can situate stocks within that umbrella definition.

When considering financial markets, the equities market comes to mind. In short, the equity market is synonymous with the stock market. While you could use the terms interchangeably, it's worth noting that the term "equity market" encompasses everything there is to say about stocks.

In general, publicly traded stocks are the most common type of security traded in the stock market. In this context, a security is a financial instrument with a monetary value attached to it. These financial instruments are usually represented by a certificate of some sort, which has a face value on it. While the face value of the document does not necessarily reflect its market value, the underlying asset that is represented by this certificate can be traded in any way. Hence, this is where the term "security" is applied.

Another example of a security is a bond. A bond is a debt security which can also be bought and sold in an open market. So, the term "security" applies to both stocks and bonds. However, for the sake of clarity, we will refer to stocks and bonds separately, as opposed to bunching them together under one definition.

That being said, it is also important to note that stock trading happens 24 hours a day, as there are various stock exchanges throughout the world. This means that, when markets are closed in America, markets are open in Asia and Europe. Nevertheless, markets do close for the weekend and holidays. Yet, traders are consistently working on deals, even when markets are closed.

In addition to equities, there are other markets that fall within the financial markets umbrella, such as commodities, currencies, and derivatives. These markets all have different dynamics and are subject to different mechanics, as the assets trading are different from the stock market. Given that these are different markets, investors need to become aware of how they work and the nuances that accompany these types of investments.

How Does the Stock Market Work?

This is a common question.

In essence, the stock market works just like any other market. This means that buyers and sellers come together to trade securities.

The core of this buying and selling process is price.

The only way that a transaction can take place is when both buyer and seller can agree on a price. When both sides agree on the price, a trade may take place. Otherwise, a lack of agreement will result in the breakdown of negotiations.

It is important to keep in mind that price is essentially set by supply and demand. This is known as "price discovery". The way price discovery works is based upon what buyers are willing to pay for a stock. While sellers may also have a fixed position regarding price, the fact

of the matter is that markets are almost always driven by buyers.

Consequently, price discovery is the mechanism that drives all financial markets, so bear in mind that something is worth what someone else is willing to pay for it.

The mechanics of price discovery imply that markets are free to fluctuate. Thus, if an individual stock is hot, then its price will go up. If the stock is cold, then its price will fall.

So, what goes into determining price?

Price discovery is a psychological condition that depends on a number of factors.

For instance, the book value of a stock is its value based on the accounting practices of that company. So, the standard "assets (-) liabilities = equity" equation is perfectly applicable in this context. The resulting value for this equation, or the equity, divided by the number of outstanding shares belonging to that company will determine the company's book value.

Take this example:

ASSETS (-) LIABILITIES = EQUITY, so,

$100 (-) $50 = $50.

In this example, the equity for this company is 50. Now, let's consider 100 outstanding shares, and we get a book value for each share of 0.50 (50 / 100 = 0.50). We can assume that each share is worth 50 cents.

Now, does that mean that each share of this company will trade at 50 cents apiece?

Not necessarily.

In fact, this is where price discovery comes in.

Let's assume that the company is "hot"—that is, it pays out a considerable dividend. Based on the expectation of this dividend, investors may be willing to pay above the book value for each share. Let's assume that investors are willing to pay $1 for each share.

Therefore, the $1 valuation for each share is the market value for this stock. In other words, it is what investors are willing to pay and not what it is actually worth.

There is one thing to be said about price discovery: no matter what the market value of a stock is, investors will keep anteing up the value, as long as they feel that there is someone else who is willing to pay even more. That is why price discovery is primarily a psychological phenomenon, often rooted in irrational behaviors.

This is why rational and informed investors must always be vigilant and avoid falling into irrational bubbles, which only lead to artificially-inflated prices that can lead investors to lose considerable amounts of their wealth when markets take downturns.

Financial Brokers

One of the most famous players in financial markets is the broker.

Now, you might ask yourself why brokers are needed.

The answer boils down to legal regulations. In the United States, financial markets are heavily regulated by several laws, in addition to government agencies.

The Securities Act of 1933 provided the first tangible legislation which regulated the stock market. This Act was produced as a response to the stock market crash of 1929. Due to the ensuing depression, the Congress of 1933 was concerned with preventing such an event from happening again.

The Securities Act paved the way for further legislation, which led to the creation of the Securities and Exchange Commission (henceforth known as the SEC) as the regulatory body that governs stock trading.

The SEC has been at the front of regulating financial markets since its inception. As such, the folks who are actually trading stocks are licensed brokers who belong to duly licensed financial institutions. These institutions, usually banks, must comply with the legal provisions of the applicable legislation, in order to be granted licensing. The individuals who work for these brokerage institutions are the individually licensed stock brokers.

Therefore, it is not the general public that buys and sells stocks, but rather it is the brokers who do all the trading. What brokerage institutions end up doing is being an intermediary in the transactions that happen on the trading floor.

With the advent of computer-based trading, the need for human brokers has decreased, as software and algorithms have been programmed to carry out many of the functions that human brokers generally conduct.

So, when the average investor is looking to put some money toward an investment, what they are really doing is giving their funds to a broker, who then uses it to make trades. This is important to keep in mind, especially in the case of investment vehicles, such as mutual funds or exchange traded funds (ETFs).

In addition, financial brokerage institutions offer the services of professional portfolio managers who take funds from individual investors and manage them in such a way as to maximize their returns. This is especially true in those cases where investors look to have a more passive role, whereby they avoid having to actually manage money themselves but rather place their trust in an institution which will take care of things for them.

Stock Exchanges and Stock Indices

The actual trading of stocks and other financial instruments takes place in a stock exchange. These exchanges are physical locations where brokers meet and conduct business. In the past, brokers had to come together face to face, in order to carry out negotiations and transactions.

Over time, technology facilitated this process. For example, orders could be telephoned in to the broker and then placed on the trading floor. With the advent of computers, trading became more automatized and conducted in real time.

Nevertheless, brokers must still maintain a presence on the trading floor. So, you will find that these institutions have offices located in the physical buildings where the trading takes place. As a result, the need for actual human brokers has decreased, given the rise of computer-based trading. While brokers are still very much alive and kicking, there just aren't that many of them anymore.

Perhaps the most famous stock exchange in the world is the New York Stock Exchange, located on Wall Street in New York City. This is home to much of the trading in the United States, though there are other stock exchanges in cities such as Chicago, Boston, Miami and Philadelphia.

But this is just the case of American cities. There are stock exchanges in various cities throughout the world, such as London, Tokyo, Shanghai, and Toronto, to name a few. This is why stock trading takes place 24 hours a day. So, when one stock exchange is closing down for the day, there are others which are just getting started.

In general, the only financial market which is open 24 hours a day, 365 days a year is the FOREX market. This market deals with the exchange of foreign currencies. Since business is always being conducted in some part of the world, then there always is a need for money. In addition, currency exchange happens every single day of the year, as bank operations never stop, even when there might be a bank holiday in their respective countries.

One very important consideration is that companies' stocks are traded in the stock exchange in which they are registered. Generally speaking, companies will be traded on the stock exchange of the country where they are based. So, a German-based company would be traded on the DAX, the German stock market.

While this isn't necessarily a rule, it is a common practice. In addition, companies which are based in countries which do not have a stock market of their own may choose to be publicly traded on stock exchanges of other countries.

In the case of US companies, they are traded on various stock markets. Take Microsoft, for example. It is traded on the Nasdaq. The Nasdaq is also located in New York City, but it is separate from the New York Stock Exchange. Therefore, if an investor wanted to purchase Microsoft stock, they would have to work with a broker who is registered on the Nasdaq, in order to make the trade.

Some companies, due to fiscal reasons, may be based in one country but be traded on a different country's stock exchange. While this isn't very common, it does happen on certain occasions when both countries' regulations allow it.

Consequently, it is important to become familiar with the various stock exchanges, not just in the United States but around the world, in order to get a feel for the way markets are behaving and developing at any given point.

One other important consideration regarding the stock market is a stock index.

You might have heard of the Dow Jones, the aforementioned Nasdaq, or the S&P 500. These are called stock indices, because they are a means of tracking the performance of individual companies. Since there are thousands of publicly-traded companies, it is hard to keep up with every one of them. So, for practical purposes, investment professionals have created such indices.

Take the Dow Jones, for example. This index tracks the performance of the 30 largest publicly-traded companies in the United States. They are all listed on the New York Stock Exchange. In the Dow Jones, you will find companies like McDonald's, Walmart, Procter and Gamble, Intel, Apple, and IBM, to name a few. These are truly the heavy hitters in this lineup.

The purpose of a stock index is to track the collective performance of these companies as a means of helping investors visualize stocks in a much easier fashion. One very important application of stock indices is that investors can purchase funds known as "index funds". Index funds are collectives in which various investors can pool their money. Then, the financial brokerage institution can use that money and invest it exclusively in the companies which are tracked on that stock exchange.

By investing in an index, investors and brokers can attempt to gain returns above the market average. In addition, index funds also help investors visualize the companies in which they are investing. This allows investors to gain confidence in the job done by portfolio or money managers.

While it is possible for investors to purchase stock in a single company, most investors choose to avoid buying stocks of a single company, due to the risk this involves. In essence, it is putting all of your eggs in a single basket. Astute investors will choose to diversify their investments by allocating their funds across various companies and various financial instruments.

As such, diversification is used as a strategy to hedge against risk. In short, hedging means that investors are looking to reduce the amount of risk that is generated by one company versus another.

For example, if an investor takes $100 and invests in Company A, the investor will lose $10 is there is a 10% reduction in the price of that stock. Now, assume the same investor takes $50 and puts it into Company A and $50 into Company B, then the 10% drop will only represent a $5 loss. Consequently, if Company B increases by 10%, then it will increase in value by $5. In this case, the drop and the increase offset each other, leaving the investor with the same $100.

In this example, the investor lost on one side and gained on the other. Thus, in the end, the investor did not lose anything. This is why diversification is a useful tool in hedging against risk. If the investor had sunk all of their funds into a single stock, the degree of risk would have been much greater, as opposed to diversifying.

Primary and Secondary Markets

When companies are incorporated—that is, they become legal entities—they are private companies. This means that the only way an individual may purchase stock in the company is if they purchase new stock issues, or if an existing stockholder sells their shares.

However, a private company may choose to "go public" and register with a stock exchange. This is called an initial public offering, or IPO. When an IPO happens, the stock of that company is traded for the first time on the public market. The IPO is underwritten by a financial institution and insured by a risk management entity.

When the IPO goes through, there is usually a line of investors waiting to get in on the first round of trading, especially if the company has potential to generate considerable returns.

Once the IPO's first round goes through, the remaining trades that go on among investors take part in the secondary market. So, the primary market happens when companies sell stock directly to investors, while the secondary, or aftermarket, happens when investors trade among themselves.

In such cases, it is important to bear in mind that investors who get into IPOs, right at the beginning, potentially can make a killing. However, those investors are generally the high-powered investors who have large amounts of capital. In this case, such investors have the cash and the credit to make, or break, large-scale deals.

Furthermore, there are investment firms called "hedge funds" who generally have vast amounts of investable funds. These so-called hedge funds, which are generally a club of wealthy investors, may scoop an entire IPO and then sell once the stock's price has risen.

One other way in which investors can purchase stock, and even bypass brokers, is to purchase stock directly from the company. This is called an over-the-counter operation. While rather uncommon, it is done when companies pledge their stock to individual investors. Often, these individual investors may be hedge funds, though it is possible that very wealthy individuals with ties to the company itself get participation in an over-the-counter operation.

Ultimately, it is certainly worth doing further research and learning about the way the markets work and how market shifts can impact your investment strategy. The most important thing is that investing in stocks is an ongoing process which requires a considerable amount of time and effort.

As we will see in upcoming chapters, learning about stock markets can become easier when you take advantage of the information and analytics tools out there, often available for a subscription fee, and which are accessible to virtually anyone.

Chapter 10 Mindset

Day traders have specific character traits that make them prosperous and able to handle the stress that comes from dealing with the stock market and the fast-paced environment. It is not a secret that this job is hard and stressful, but what is a secret are the character traits that are needed by a broker so that they do not crack under pressure. 90% of the investors who trade on the stock market as a day trader will not make it.

Traits That Set You Apart from Those That Have Failed

Winning traders have several character traits that help them be successful. Below, I will go over a few of these traits that can set you apart from those that have failed miserably.

Rise Early and Shine

Waking up at an early time is very crucial to your day trading abilities. You do not want to rush your routine for your pre-trading hours. When doing day trading, you are able to make quick decisions when faced with pressure, and it is very crucial for you to be fully awake as well as an alert when the market opens. When you go on a walk an hour prior to working, this will increase your endorphins and give you a natural high that will carry you through the day with extra energy. This gets your blood moving and helps you get alert quickly.

Prior to the Market, Do Some Research

If you have stocks that have just been added to your watch list, then you will need to do the research prior to the market opening. To trade a stock, you should be fully informed about why it is moving. Being inadequately prepared can show up in how you trade for that day. You should trade with confidence and a little less uncertainty, especially if you prepare yourself completely prior to investing or trading the stocks.

You need to know the key support levels as well as the intraday resistance that is listed on the charts daily.

Ensure That Trade Plans Are Followed

Prepare a plan for all the scenarios that could arise with the stocks that are on your watch list. They are well informed of where they will stop out, enter, and take profits all before they enter for the trade. Without a trading plan, you will be more stressed out, and it will present as a more difficult accomplishment. You will need to prepare in advance.

Investors Know That Trading Every Day Is Not Necessary

A winning trader can tell you that every day will not be positive, and some days are not good for trading opportunities. If you cannot recognize these days, then you will fail. When trading, you can win or lose, knowing when to step back is necessary.

To grow your account, it's just as much about avoiding the losses as well as the wins. Recognize the criteria that make it an A+ stock opportunity. This helps you to recognize when to sit on your hands.

Reflect on the Trades That You Have Purchased

If it does not get measured, then it does not get improved. Successful traders will track their trades religiously. Examine the wins and see what each one has that connects them. Then, use that analysis to replicate this for future purchases. For those trades that are losses, you will need to analyze the common connections and avoid making those same mistakes. Eliminate the habits which lead you to the losing trade, which is outside your plan of trading. Not every single losing trade is an actual bad trade. It is unavoidable for a losing trade not to happen, so remember that it will happen—just make sure you are prepared for it. If you lose due to a rule of trading, then you will need to figure out why, and then you can make changes to prevent it from continuing to happen. Now that I have gone over ways that successful day traders stay successful, I will discuss other ways that show the mentality of a successful day trader and how to fix the mental game that is helping them increase their profitability.

Small Losses Happen — Embrace Them

When working as a day trader, you will deal with losses. This is customary; however, you need to be able to handle it. Losses can impact your emotional stability, and it can make a big dent in your confidence. You must recognize the triggers that lead to loss and can create a revenge trade, as well as some micro-managing that will influence us to make improper procedure changes or even dump a stock that we should hold on to. By embracing small losses, you will be able to fix the trigger of loss. A small loss simply means that you are testing the waters and doing something right. If the losses are sandwiched between some bigger wins, you will be able to handle them easier.

Consider Your Next 100 Trades

Many traders can live or die by the actions of their trades, or the need to make their next trade. Over long-term trade should be analyzed for the overall focus, and this should not be connected to the gains or losses of that time period, but the overall time period that you own the stock.

Do not stress out because of the loss that you receive. In the grand picture of building your trading portfolio, one loss can be meaningless. Instead, consider obsessing about those 100 trades that come next. This can keep you focused on something that is not pertinent. The short-term is what you should be focusing on; however, you would be focusing on the process. When trading for probability, you will experience losses for good trades. If you experience a drawdown, then you are not poorly trading your stocks. Do not let a positive trade with short terms that are poor impact the results of the psychology of the trade.

Reduce Your Risks to Fight Back the Fear

Placing trades can be scary. When you place your cash in the hands of another, you are stressed and worried. It is hard to trust that you will not lose it. Anyone that has been practicing trading, who then goes out on their own, must know how it feels to fear losing money. Fear can manifest into your trading strategy and keep you in a losing streak. It makes it harder to pull the trigger on a trade than it would be if you were not so fearful. Reduce your risk if fear is showing up for you when trying to trade. If your loss is small, then you will be less scared to trade. If your normal risk is $200 per trade, then you will need to have a lower $100 trade to feel less pressure and fear. Once you start to do this without fear, you can increase your trade amount by up to $200 again. All these tips show how the mental psyche of a day trader works its best. You also need to put into context things that can negatively affect the day trader within his own mindset belief system. Below, I have included several mindset beliefs that can affect how the day trader will negatively impact their trading accouterment.

Fear That They Are Missing Some Great Move

As a day trader, they are conditioned to stalk the market for fear of missing some big break; however, they become more like a two-year-old who does not want to go to bed. They sit and sit, with fear that they will miss some amazing experience that will take place on the market. They fear that while they are away, the market will continue to run without them, and this creates anxiety about the loss of opportunity. Due to this fear, the day trader may find themselves jumping into a buy simply because he fears the loss. This can also happen when the market does free-fall.

This is an easy-to-notice point on the chart with the high or low within the print of the day. It is just not enough, even $250. The day trader is churning out a profit of $250 a day from his $10,000 account. This is due to his steady strategy and system that he has been implementing; although he is managing and trading for the good, he is not happy. He considers that $250 is not enough and that $500 would be much better for him. This is the point that greed becomes the deciding factor in his future profits. At this point, greed takes the wheel and starts to decide what to buy and when to sell. This creates a trigger in his brain that ripples into making all kinds of trading mistakes. He overtrades and stops sticking to his parameters.

He experiences rampant emotions that resemble an angry football enthusiast, such as yelling at the screen. This is the culminating downfall of a lot of day traders. This is the time that a day trader will refuse a profit of $300 simply because it is not bigger and better. At this point, his winning trades start to turn into losing trades, and his $10,000 account decreases to $5,000 in a matter of months.

The Loving Feeling That Those Who Succeed Experience and Now Create a Need to Continue That Feeling

For instance, let's say that the day trader has an amazing day on the market. Everything is going their way. They are having episodes of minimal stress elevation. This day is amazing in all ways.

This overwhelming feeling of joy and warmth can create a feeling that is addictive. The day trader rarely feels this kind of emotional high, so they try to recreate it over and over again. They begin to add to their already existing positions. They double and triple the investment. This is similar to many who are super happy with his family. He enjoys their company, and it brings him boundless joy. He decides that he needs to feel this more, so he heads out to find another family to add to his already existing joy. As we all know, this can only end badly, so the resulting factor of over joyful and ecstatic for a day trader can create a need to feel that over and over again and loses it all trying to reach that high. So how can you use these negative triggers to your advantage? Below, I have included a breakdown of how to use this to your advantage, whether it is you who are experiencing these emotions or someone else you trade with.

When someone losses in a trade, the money from the trade simply goes to another trader's account. What this means is that these negative emotional, mental blocks can become your payday.

Use Your Excitement for Good

Instead of doubling or tripping down your investment, create a double stop to block these urges. This can be used in many ways. For instance, consider how much time you could spend in a private villa on a tropical island. Then, place your trailing point stop 2 for 20 contracts. Then, double the size of the position you are currently in. This means that as long as that trade is going higher, you will stay; however, if the market turns, I am removed from the position with a nice profit, and I get short on contracts that total 10.

This will use the market dynamics for emotions and take a clear and clean advantage. This sell-off will only occur from the trades of another day that succumbed to the emotional reactions for buying at the top because they feared losing out on the move altogether. It can also be contributed to the fear of missing the euphoria that you get in a win and when you have that winning position. After the market turns, the day traders that bought will be the fuel that needs to move down, and they will dump the position once the loss is too great.

Consider What a Newbie Would Do and Then Snatch Them at the Low

Visualize what the newbie day trader would be doing at this exact position. For instance, you entered at a specific point, at what point is the pain point for a newbie? If the S&P movement was 6 points with no retracements that were meaningful, then this would become UNCLE for the majority of day traders. Imagine that this is the pain point of the newbie, and after this point, swoop in and buy up the stocks.

Look for Those Ticks

Watch for those ticks that will come along. If the readings are over +1000 tick readings or -1000 tick readings below, then you will need to fade out your moves. If there is a +1000 tick move and I have already gone, then I start to exit the move with a short position. However, the reverse of this is also true for a stopping point of 4 ½ and a target point of 3. If neither is hit after 25 minutes, exit this trade at the price that is current.

High Five Equals Sell

When I see traders going around the room giving others a high five for a good trade, I take that as my cue to sell.

This is a signal that I have noticed comes from extreme emotional euphoria and means that the market is in a good spot.

Traits That Will Ensure You Succeed as a Day Trader

So how can you ensure that you will be successful at day trading? And what does it take to be successful? There are 3 psychological quirks that will have an enormous impact on your day trading. As a day trader, we can face some troubling problems, and most of these are going to be ones that we do not even know we have. Some of our human characteristics will affect how we trade and, in the end, our bottom line. Although there are several that can affect us, the five most important and detrimental are listed below, with a breakdown of how they do affect us with our day trading. These can place a block in the way of us achieving the goals that we have set for our finances.

There Are Several Enemies That We Do Not Even Recognize and Most of It Is Ourselves

When you deal with day trading, there will be moments that we will err, and this can be fixed, but only if we analyze it and make attempts to adjust the err. If you have exited from a trade too early, you will find that by adjusting your criteria, you will be able to make a better decision. Make adjustments to this error by looking for an indicator that is different or takes a longer amount of time to make the trade. If your trading strategy is solid, but you still find yourself losing some money, you will need to examine yourself and the psychology that we apply to the solution. When dealing with your own inner workings, your view is often skewed due to being so personally connected. You may not have the ability to fix the problem that is creating the loss. Your true problem could be created by a clouded mindset that is biased at best. There may be some trivialities that are superficial, and they are creating the discrepancies within your trading ability. For example, you have a trading strategy but never stick to it. So, this person is on a continuous adjustment period, and nothing is working because it is not given the proper time to work nor the right amount of credit. By sticking with a strategy, you will be able to check your resolve for solving the equation.

Your success record will increase by applying one specific approach that has a solid framework and foundation.

There Is Power in Awareness

Being aware of the possibilities that could be creating the issues will help us to adjust them later. By creating actions which we can adjust over time, we can begin to see how each action is creating loss and change the habits that are contributing to this loss. We will overcome the problems that arise and be able to eliminate these problems. Since there is no magic plan that will make everyone a winner, this is where knowing who you are and adjust non-serving traits will come in handy. Psychology states that by being aware of our pitfalls, we can adjust them and improve upon who we are. This rings true for the day trader as well. Changing our habits and creating a profit will help us to be better at our day trading.

Bias Sensory-Derived

By compiling information from the experiences around us, we gain opinions, and this can create a bias with which will dictate how we operate. This will allow the investor to function as well as learn behaviors. However, as we understand that this is forming behaviors or opinions that would be factual in bases and evidence shows, it is often not the case. For instance, a trader who watches the news and bases his knowledge on the reports will believe he has stripped the opinions from the broadcaster and is going on pure facts when he, in fact, is not. If our sources are all biased, then how can we expect our own thoughts and opinions not to be biased based. There are always two sides to every story, and biased is the basis with which these stories have differences.

Constant exposure to a biased opinion can, in turn, make you believe that this biased opinion is your own truth, even if it is not factual. Those raised to believe that dogs are scary will, no matter what, always believe that dogs are scary even if there are no bases for the truth. Since there is no counterevidence to dispute the bias, the opinion becomes their truth as it is the only available information that has heard, even if it is biased.

Vagueness and Ambiguity Are Avoided

This can also be known as the fear of the unknown. The avoidance of what is possible to occur, even if it has not. The avoidance of things that is not clear to our thoughts. This avoidance can prevent even a seasoned investor from doing things that would increase their profit line and keep them locked in that state of loss. Some traders have actually found that they fear the process of making money, and this rings true for many entrepreneurs as well.

This is not a conscious fear; it is something that is deep within. The fear of the taxes that they will owe can be so daunting that they will fear themselves into losses. Expanding the zone with which they are comfortable can create blocks and worry that sends them into downward spirals of loss. This creates patterns of sabotage that is done by self. This can also create a bias about which industry they will enter, making them fear trading in any other industry than the one they are most familiar with. The fact that this industry is declining will be irrelevant to them. They will simply continue to pump money into a dead horse. They avoid the chance of winning a profit by staying in familiar investments and associate this with uncertainty.

This can also be seen when the investor holds onto winners less time than they should and sells the loser way later than they should have. If the price fluctuates, they struggle to face the facts of the movement and then fail at determining the appropriate action. They also will fear the experience of loss and begin to make drastic and risky decisions that will place them in jeopardy of losing it all. When they deviate from the rational, they will then become irrational and start acting accordingly. This then causes the investor to miss the gains that potentially could make them increase their wealth.

The Anticipation Is Tangible

Anticipation is immensely powerful and can create stress as well as worry and excitement. Since anticipation is connected to "I want" or "I need," the mentality is self-serving. Most of the time, our anticipations will take place way in the future, and sometimes, they will take place within a few weeks. Although these can be far in the future, they create an emotional enjoyment that becomes addicting. This addiction can become the focus of how we want to feel always, and this becomes the achievement instead of the reaction. This can limit our ability to see that the payout is now and block us from taking the payment with anticipation that there is a bigger one coming, and eventually, we lose the money altogether or make ways less than we should have. Easy money can find its way to our door.

It is more than likely that it will be grabbed by the ones that think calm and collected about their trading values. We can begin to fall into an anticipatory feeling that becomes the consolation and not the reaction to the prize. Watching the changing of hands for billions of dollars can be exciting, but if the confidence is not there, we can miss our opportunity to benefit from this changing of hands. This is like us subconsciously telling ourselves that we are better off dreaming and that this dream is better than the real thing. Wanting to become profitable has become the goal instead of actually being profitable. By understanding what is affecting our trading, we can begin to make changes for the better. The psychology of day trading can be an extensive research project in and of itself, but awareness of how we respond and what our actions are can bring us to understand better why we are at this point. One way to adjust our psychology is to remove the bias that is influencing our decisions.

Use charts, since they do not lie. Remain objective and become focused on the strategies that will bring profit instead of the movement of price. Avoid others' well-thought-out opinions and create some of your own. Gain knowledge of how the market moves and shakes. This will help you overcome the fear and the greed that will arise during a day trading career. Unknown territory can create mistakes, so avoid the unknown by researching and gaining knowledge. Base all of our actions on an objectively sound decision that is made with knowledge instead of fear.

Chapter 11 Rules That Help to Reduce Your Risks in the Stock Market

As a beginner in the stock market, it is important that you learn some of the best ways to reduce your risk. The stock market can be a good way to make money, but many beginners will fall prey to some of the mistakes that make this a really big risk. There is enough risk in the investment on its own, so you need to find ways to reduce your risks to make as much money as possible. Some of the steps that you can take to ensure that you are getting the most out of your investment include:

Do not follow the crowd

When you decide to get into stock market investing, you must learn how to make decisions on your own. It is tempting to always listen to your broker or to listen to the friend who has been on the market for a long time. While it is just fine for you to take the advice of others when you are getting started, you must remember that this is your investment. No one else has money on the line when you pick a certain stock or go with a certain strategy - only you do.

What this means is that you can still ask for advice and suggestions from other people. Talking to your broker and some friends who may know the market a little bit better is fine. However, take everything with a grain of salt. You will run into troubles if you hear what someone else says and then jump right in without even thinking about the investment. Always do your own research and use your own judgment to figure out which investments are the best for you.

Pick out a strategy and always stick with it

As you should know by now, there are a lot of different strategies that you can work with when it is time to invest in the stock market. All of these strategies have the potential of making you money, but you need to make sure that you fully understand the strategy that you are working with. If you are not using the method in the proper way, you will not be able to make money.

You also need to make sure that when you pick a strategy, you are sticking with that strategy the whole time. It is easy for a beginner to see a new approach that they think is good, but then try to switch right in the middle of a trade because it is not going the way that they want. This is dangerous. You are never going to succeed when you are splitting up two strategies. There are times, no matter which strategy that you pick, where you are not going to make money, and that is okay. You should just leave the market and call it good, rather than losing more money because you tried to switch your game plan.

You may be tempted to switch out your strategy because you do not fully understand how to manage itor because you start losing money. However, the second that you try to switch during a trade, the harder it will be to make money and keep your investment safe. You can always switch out strategies when the trade is done if you do not like using the one you picked, but stick it out until the trade is done.

Forget about the timing

Timing the market is never a good idea. There are a lot of beginners who will try to figure out how to time the stock market, but they often end up losing a lot of money rather than earning anything. Experts in all industries agree that it is pretty much impossible to find the exact tops and exact bottoms of a stock, and if you happen to reach them, it was because you are lucky, not because of good planning.

The issue here is that you can't predict how other people will react to a market. You can make some good guesses, but it is impossible to tell for certain when people will start selling or buying a particular stock. If you are trying to buy at the exact lowest point and then sell at the exact highest point, you will miss out on a lot of great opportunities. What you need to focus on instead is finding when the stock is at a good discount for your purchase and then selling the stock when it gets above its market value. This may not give you maximum profit, but you will earn a profit, and it helps you to avoid staying in the market too long.

Some financial advisors insist that timing the market is the only way that you can make a good profit in the stock market. The issue with this is that this strategy is often going to backfire on you. Additionally, while it affects you quite a bit, it will have no effect on the advisor. If you spend too much of your time trying to outsmart the market, you will be the one who loses.

Only invest what you can afford

When you see a good investment opportunity, it is tempting to jump in and use all the money that you have. You may go out and use all your savings and some of the money from your paychecks this month in the hopes that it will turn out well and you will become rich. But what happens if the investment doesn't go the way that you plan? Now you have nothing, and you may not even be able to pay your bills the next month.

One of the best practices that you can do when you get started with stock investing is that you only invest the money that you would be comfortable with losing. No one wants to lose money on an investment, but it is something that can happen. If you go into the market assuming that you will never lose, you are setting yourself up for a lot of trouble. Perhaps you should consider setting up a savings account ahead of time and putting some money in to help you with your investments without worrying that you are investing too much. No matter which method you choose to go with, make sure that you only add in the amount of money to the investment that wouldn't be disastrous if you end up losing.

Keep your expectations realistic

There are a lot of beginners who will join the stock market and hope that they are able to make a lot of money. They may hear that it is possible to lose money in this market, but they figure that they can outsmart the market and that they will not end up losing all that much in the process. However, this is a bad way to enter the market. Even seasoned stock market investors who have been doing this for years will still lose money. There are many times when the market does something that you do not expect, and you can lose money no matter how much you plan.

In addition, going into the market and thinking you will earn money overnight is a bad idea. Some investments could potentially make you rich, but these are really risky. It is unlikely that you will actually succeed because the risk is so high, and you will most likely lose more money than you can afford to lose.

Going into the stock market is risky enough. Do not make it worse by going into the market with expectations that are not all that realistic. Understand that you can make some money in this investment, but it will often take some time to see that success. You must also understand that there are some times, no matter how hard you plan ahead, when you will end up losing money in the process.

Keep the emotions out of the game

You also need to make sure that you are able to keep emotions out of the game. As soon as those emotions come into play, you will start losing money. These emotions will often lead you to make poor decisions, and you are more likely to lose out on your investment.

This is why having a good strategy in place will make all the difference when it comes to making money with the stock market. This strategy will set up all the rules that you need to follow. It will tell you when to enter the market when you should leave the market, and all the steps in between. It basically outlines what you need to do, taking most of the decisions out of the game and allowing you to keep your emotions away as well.

One thing that you must learn to avoid at all costs is revenge trading. This starts when you end up losing some money on one trade because you made bad decisions or the market did not react the way that you wanted. Instead of just taking the loss and learning from it, you decide that you need to start making that money back right away. You go into risky investment options in the hopes of earning that money back quickly. Often investors who choose to go with revenge trading will not think through their decisions. The only thinking that they do is that they want to earn the money back. They will pick bad investments and not listen to the advice of others along the way. Because of this, they often lose a ton more money than they would have if they just learned from the mistake and moved on.

If you are someone who is really emotional or can let their decisions be affected by what is going on around them, or if you are worried about losing money in the process of trading, then investing in the stock market may not be the right choice. There are times when the market will not behave the way that you want, and there isn't much you can do about it. For these kinds of people, there are a lot of other investments, including ones that are less risky, that can help you earn good money as well.

Set your stop points

Another thing that you can consider doing is to set up some stop points. These are basically the points when you will exit the market, both when you are making profits and when you are losing. These can help to minimize your risks because you will make the decisions about these stop points before you enter the market and money is at stake. If you forget to do these, it can sometimes be hard to get out of the market at the right time, no matter how much logic you use.

The first stop point that you need to set is the one where you will exit the market when you are losing money. While you never want to think about losing money, it is much better to do this before you put any money in. This stop point should be at a place where you would still be comfortable with losing that money if things go wrong. Then, as soon as the market reaches that point, you will exit the market, no matter what may happen later on.

Some beginners find that it is tempting to stay in the market, even when they are losing money. They figure that the market will return and that they will be able to recoup their losses if they just stay in. This rarely ever works, and if you keep in the market, you are likely to keep losing money. With this stop point, you can keep your losses to a minimum and re-enter the market later on if you decide to.

You should also consider adding in a stop point to exit when you have made enough profits. Yes, it would be nice to plan for unlimited profits, but this is not going to happen, no matter which industry you choose to invest in. Adding this stop point in will ensure that you get some profit. Without it, you may be tempted to stay in the market too long, and when the market turns, you may end up losing all that profit and more.

It is best to set up these stop points ahead of time for each trade before you invest any money into the market. This will ensure that you are making logical decisions, long before the emotions can come into play, and you will be surprised at what a difference it can make in the amount of profit that you enjoy with this investment.

Chapter 12 The History of the Stock Market

To understand the history of the stock market, we should have a grasp of the inner workings of a stock exchange first—specifically the bid-ask spread that also influences prices of shares. The bid-ask spread is a sort of register that consolidates the demand and supply of a stock in a central position. On the one hand, it allows people who need to buy stocks to place an order of the number and price of shares they intend to buy. On the other, it gives the sellers an opportunity to list the number of shares they intend to sell, as well as the target price for them. The final price of the stock depends on whether the buyer is willing to settle for the price of the buyer or whether the buyer is able to buy the stocks at their listed price. The laws of demand and supply also come into play, with buyers being forced to increase their purchase price when the competition is higher and sellers accepting a lower price for their stocks if there are not enough buyers to drive demand and price up.

Now, the stock exchange facilitates this conversion of ownership from the seller to the buyer by bringing them together in one platform. It is essentially a platform comprising of stockbrokers where they congregate to perform the business of exchanging (buying and selling) stocks. But who exactly runs the stock exchange? The stock exchanges as they currently exist were founded so long ago that the issue of who owns them seems immaterial. For the most part, the stock exchange is just the building or platform on which brokers buy and sell. The most important aspect of the stock exchange is the stocks that are listed in it. And because companies only list where they can be sure of attracting investors (stockholders), this is a very important aspect of their operations. It is no surprise, therefore, that the oldest bourses were started as corporations by stockbrokers to facilitate the exchange of securities among themselves.

The stock market has had a long and eventful history, one that is almost as long as the banking industry, by far the oldest financial institution still surviving today.

1100s–1400s

The earliest versions of the stock market were rather different from the bourse as we know it today. In France, the country of origin for this early stock exchanges, *courretiers de change* agents oversaw the agricultural debts issued by banks to farmers all over the state. They could swap and renegotiate these debts, an equity exchange that formed the foundation for the current stock market. Over time, the business of exchanging debts grew, and these men expanded to new markets, including government securities. As the first stockbrokers, the Venetian *courtiers de change* established stocks as a legitimate way for "common" people to make money in the financial markets.

Interestingly, these men carried on a system of cross-transactions with each other, buying debt and equity of each other based on risk and various other factors. Because they represented different banks in the debt issuance and collection sector, this interlinkage would later evolve to become the present-day interbank lending system, whereby banks issue each other with cheaper short-term loans. The people involved in this trade were mostly commodity traders, with the value of commodities changing hands but not the commodities themselves. This was a virtualization of the business functions that was way ahead of its time at the time.

The merchants of Venice started trading in government securities in the early thirteenth century. They were soon followed by banks in Verona, Genoa, Florence, and Pisa as it became evident that government securities presented a wonderful investment opportunity. Trading between the merchants was done by word of mouth and handwritten agreements. The extent of organized trading was limited to the houses of prominent traders where many of these *courretiers de change* could congregate and negotiate terms and conduct their transactions.

From France, the development of the securities market moved to Belgium and Netherlands, where traders started stock markets in Antwerp, Bruges, Ghent, and Rotterdam between the 1400s and the 1500s. In Antwerp, a clan of traders named the Van der Beurze family established a hub for stock traders to exchange equities, forming the first formalized stock market, except it still traded in agricultural debts, commodities, and government bonds. The concept of private companies using the stock markets to raise money had not yet been born.

1500s–1700s

In the meantime, before the first publicly traded company made it into the bourse, England joined in the "stock" trading enterprise. As usual, government securities were the main commodities traded, but debts and commodities also changed hands. By this time, as European civilizations continued to expand, there was a stock market in pretty much every country that had a banking industry. Business ownership also started to change, with partnerships and corporations becoming increasingly popular as businessmen recognized the profit of combining their financial muscle. New philosophies of a business organization birthed the limited liability system of business organization and paved the way for the modern conglomerate.

The first publicly traded company would emerge from an unexpected area: risk. At a time when the Western world was discovering the rest of the world and venturing out to explore it, merchant ships were making many traders extremely rich. Explorers had discovered the West Indies as a land filled with business opportunities and tremendous riches, but the sea routes they took exposed them to piracy, with numerous voyages turning up zero returns because a ship was ransacked at sea. In fact, losing a ship meant that the trader who had put up the money for the voyage, including the commodities to be bartered for gold and other treasure, wound up losing a ton of money.

To reduce the risk of losing a merchant ship at sea, a group of traders formed the East India Company, with each owning a portion of the assets but shielded from personal liability for any losses suffered beyond their investment in that particular expedition. This format of overseas trading quickly caught on. By keeping one's eggs in separate baskets, so to say, traders could have one out of three or four of their invested ships lost at sea and still end up making some money from the transaction.

As shareholding in a company became more and more liberalized, the Dutch East India Company became, in 1602, the first publicly traded company. The shares of the company were listed in the Amsterdam Stock Exchange. Every share was entitled to an equal percentage of the proceeds of the company's profits. However, the trading of shares was not done in dedicated exchange houses. For example, the business of the New York Stock Exchange was conducted in coffee shops. Brokers would meet in coffee shops and conduct their business there, but this soon proved to be too ineffective, and the business of trading shares was moved into the stock exchanges.

The systems that even today moderate stock trading were put in place back then, enabling the traders to physically identify the person with the shares they wanted, approach them, and negotiate to buy them off. The counter was soon discovered to be a better alternative to tracking down traders with a particular stock. People intending to sell would just list their shares at the counter, and people wanting to buy would place their orders at the counter. An easy and effective system of centralized control was established, but having a centralized buy/sell counter meant that the market forces of demand and supply were also let loose. Someone with a stock could wait until so many orders had been placed that they could name their price, however exorbitant, and get a buyer. The book value of the stock, which had been the only moderating factor before trading floors and counters were opened up, was no longer the sole determinant of the value at which the stock would sell anymore.

Even though the Amsterdam Stock Exchange was the first to have a publicly listed company, the London Stock Exchange quickly gained prominence as the foremost bourse in Europe, bolstered by the spirited expansion of the British Empire. When the stock markets started, they were simply a congregation of businessmen who sought to establish a better working environment for their activities dealing in agricultural debt and other commodities. The progression to trading in the shares of companies happened over a few hundred years. But even with this growth, the full potential of the stock market was not realized by the government or the investors themselves. While the usefulness of stockholding to reduce risk and make business more profitable was recognized, the effect that this particular institution would have on the rest of the business institutions escaped the attention of everyone involved.

1700s–1800s

What we know as the stock market today can be said to have started at the onset of the nineteenth century when the previously unregulated stock markets worked themselves up into a bubble. The ease with which a business could raise the money to invest in infrastructure and expand its operations acted as a stimulus to other sectors of the economy. A few centuries before, the industrial revolution had transformed the whole business environment of the European continent, transforming it from an agrarian economy into an industry-based one. Even as these changes swept through the continent, the equities industry pretty much grew unregulated, with businesses being formed overnight, issuing shares with little supervision from the government and very little accountability to shareholders.

The bubble soon burst, and many listed companies could no longer afford to pay dividends to their shareholders. As the regulatory body responsible for the biggest stock exchange in the continent at the time, the government of England stepped in to mitigate the situation with a ban on listings in the London Stock Exchange that extended all the way to the year 1825. The delay allowed the New York Stock Exchange, started in 1817, to flourish. New companies that could not go public in London opted for the American bourse.

Furthermore, the NYSE was located at the epicenter of US trade and commerce, and even though it was not the first stock exchange established in the new world, it consolidated itself into the biggest and most competitive stock exchange the world over.

Modern Stock Markets

Even though governments have never been directly involved in the operations of the stock markets, regulations were enacted all through the nineteenth and twentieth century to formalize the operations of bourses even as their importance to the economy rose to greater heights. The need for corporations to raise money for expansion made it necessary for stock exchanges to be established in nearly every country by the middle twentieth century. Today, as much as one trillion worth of stocks are traded in stock exchanges around the world.

As the number of people interested in investing in the stock market increased, media attention and the need for information necessitated the formation of industry measures of stock market performance, taking into consideration the trends observed in the strongest companies in a stock exchange to estimate the overall performance of the bourse. These measures are called indexes. They include the Dow Jones, Standard & Poor, and the NASDAQ-100 among others. Specialized indexes have been formulated to measure the performance of various sectors of the economy by the performance of the stocks of companies that dominate them.

The current stock market is highly globalized. Investors in America can easily invest in Chinese companies listed in China or America and vice versa, simply because stockbrokers are allowed to trade in pretty much any stock market around the world. From international to regional indexes, progress has been directed heavily toward the global stock market as a whole. Mergers between stock exchanges have been increasing gradually since the turn of the century. The fact that stock exchanges are independent entities that are largely unregulated by state bodies in the scope of their operations allows for mergers and partnerships that have pushed the boundaries, pushing gradually toward a unified world stock market.

Stock Exchanges

As the world stock market developed, various exchanges evolved to appeal to certain industries based on the kind of stockbrokers that transact in them. A certain pattern of specialization has emerged in some of the biggest bourses, with some countries proving to be conducive to companies in certain sectors of the economy. For example, the Canadian Stock Exchange, commonly known as the TSX, has a higher number of companies in the oil and gas sector than every other bourse. Because it allows companies based in the country as well as the rest of the world to be listed and because the country, with a huge portion of the Arctic region open to it, is a leader in the oil and gas industry, these types of companies have gravitated toward a listing there.

Understanding the specialization of a stock exchange can really help you as an investor to know what exchanges to target in your hunt for stocks. In a later chapter, we shall look at the benefits of diversifying your portfolio by incorporating local and international stocks and mixing up your stocks between industries. With the stock market virtually blown open by digital technology infrastructure, you need not confine yourself to one stock exchange, even if it is the NYSE, the world's largest by market capitalization, or the NASDAQ, which ranks second.

The New York Stock Exchange

The NYSE is the leading stock exchange, not only in America but also in the world. It has the biggest market capitalization of any other stock exchange in the world. So big, in fact, that the combined value of companies listed in the NYSE is greater than the combined capitalization of the next three biggest stock exchanges. Another distinction enjoyed by the New York Stock Exchange is that it is home to 70 of the world's largest corporations, as well as accounting for over 80% of the Standard & Poor 500 Index. As part of its efforts to continue dominating the world stock market, the NYSE in 2007 merged with the Euronext to create the first truly transatlantic stock exchange.

Established in 1792 with the signing of the Buttonwood Agreement by a group of 24 stockbrokers, the bourse has grown to incorporate over 1,000 stockbrokers on the trading floor and tens of other brokers who are affiliated with partner firms. The NYSE was started at the tail end of the old stock trading world order where trading in securities was done by a loosely affiliated network of brokers in the various regions of the world. After 25 years of operating from coffee shops, the stockbrokers reorganized, instituted reforms on fair play and stock manipulation, and adopted electrical telegraph technology to increase the effectiveness of trading in 1817. They also established a dedicated building where all their transactions would be carried out—the first stock trading establishment in America. By merging with other organizations of brokers, the NYSE gradually established its dominance in the world stock market by increasing membership and trade volumes, soon overtaking the Philadelphia Stock Exchange, the oldest stock exchange in the United States by age of establishment.

The London Stock Exchange
The London Stock Exchange is the biggest stock market in England and Europe. Some of the largest companies in the continent are listed in the bourse, as well as some giants in the world stage. Even though the NYSE enjoys the distinction of being the biggest bourse in the world, the LSE is decidedly the most international of all stock markets, with companies from over 60 countries in all parts of the world listed. Companies are drawn to listing in the stock exchange because of the large pool of well-established financial institutions in the city of London that provide them with a deep and easily accessible capital pool. The LSE is also linked with the Italian stock exchange to form the London Stock Exchange Group.

Even though the LSE was founded in 1698, it wasn't until 1801 that it was formally registered as part of the effort by the government of England to bring the then extremely wayward stock market under control. For the first 25 years of its existence until 1825, the LSE was barred from listing new companies, a fact that allowed the NYSE, considerably younger and located out of Europe (then the world epicenter of finance and business) to gain an advantage and grow unchecked.

NASDAQ

In the 1970s, the dominance of the NYSE, the world's largest stock market by capitalization, was challenged by the newly formed NASDAQ stock exchange. This innovative new bourse was formed by a partnership between the National Association of Securities Dealers and the Financial Industry Regulatory Authority. It eliminated entirely the need for a physical location for a stock exchange, a building where brokers meet and exchange stocks among themselves. By using a network of computers, the NASDAQ was able to reduce the bid-ask spread and increase the effectiveness of the process substantially. Soon, the rest of the industry followed the path blazed by the NASDAQ, going electronic to increase efficiency. However, most stock exchanges have maintained the physical location of their activities, hybridizing their operations between electronic and on-the-floor trading.

Since its establishment, NASDAQ has grown in leaps and bounds and is currently the second biggest stock exchange in the world. The bourse started off as a quotation system that combined technology with stock trading to facilitate electronic transactions through the traditional on-the-floor transactions, but it gradually built its trading capabilities, eventually becoming the biggest virtual stock exchange in the world. Nasdaq Inc., the company that owns and operates NASDAQ, has proven to be quite enterprising, actively seeking mergers, partnerships, and buyouts of other stock exchanges to consolidate its operations globally. Some of its most ambitious consolidation efforts include the OMX merger in 2010 that allowed it to operate in the Nordic countries and the ultimately unsuccessful bid for the NYSE.

The Tokyo Stock Exchange

The Tokyo Stock Exchange is the largest bourse in Asia and the fourth biggest in the world based on the market cap of the companies listed. Unlike the other large stock exchanges in the world, the TSE was established with the help of the government in 1878. Up until 1942, the Tokyo Stock Exchange was just one of ten bourses that facilitated stock trading in cities across the country. In the year 1943, all the stock markets were combined into the TSE. Even though the TSE has faced some problems with its systems, it still holds a strategic position as the gateway to the Asia region and has been forming partnerships with other bourses like the LSE in the face of a highly competitive international stock market.

Euronext

In 2000, the Brussels Stock Exchange, the Paris Bourse, and the Amsterdam Stock Exchange merged to form Euronext. The merger was made possible by the synchronization of financial systems in Eurozone countries. At a €3.8 trillion valuation, the Euronext replaces the LSE as the biggest bourse in Europe and also claims its position as the fourth largest in the world.

Stock Market Crashes in History

Trading in the stock market is very emotionally driven, and sometimes public attitudes conspire to bring these markets to their knees. Some of the major stock market crashes that have started in America and affected the entire world stock markets include the Wall Street crash of 1929, the 1973–1974 crash, the crash of 1987 (which came to be known as Black Monday), the dot-com bubble burst in 2000, and the stock market crash of 2008.

The Wall Street Crash of 1929

The 1920s were a time of wealth and financial prosperity in America. In the aftermath of World War I, a spirit of great optimism abounded, with rural folk swarming to urban areas to make a better life in the ever-expanding industrial sector. Even as large-scale farming practices drove down prices and wreaked havoc in the agricultural sector, the view among the American public was that the stock market bull run that has started soon after the war would continue forever. Another cause for the bull run was widespread speculation in the stock markets.

The first sign of trouble appeared in March 1929 with a warning by the Federal Reserve on the dangers of continued speculation in the stock market. Investors started pulling their money off the stock market, but assurances by the National City Bank that people could access cheap credit offered a short respite. Even though the whole economy was sluggish with declining sales of cars, high consumer debt, a sluggish construction industry, and declining production of steel in the mills scattered around the country, the bull run continued undeterred. In fact, the Dow Jones rose over 20% between June and September to peak at 380.

From this high point, the stock market started a slow decline that many people dismissed as a healthy correction. Some pundits went as far as advising people to buy because the market would pick right up and continue with its stratospheric rise. However, events overseas created some very deep concerns. In London, a prominent British investor named Clarence Hatry was sent to prison after being found guilty of forgery with the intention to defraud. This arrest precipitated a phenomenal crash in the London stock market, which in turn jarred the confidence of American investors.

A period of great instability and heavy selling followed until October 24 or what would come to be known as Black Thursday, when the stock market declined 11% after an unprecedented morning of heavy selling. Another attempt by bankers to placate the public created another temporary respite, but this one lasted just two days. By Monday morning, the panic selling started again in real earnest. The Dow fell 13% by the end of the day and then lost another 12% points on Tuesday. By November, the Dow was down to 198 points from a high of 381 just two months before. In the end, the crash had wiped as much as $40 billion from the US economy. The country would need almost the whole of the 1930–1940 decade recovering the massive losses suffered.

The Stock Market Crash of 1973–1974

On January 9, 1973, *Time Magazine* predicted that 1973 would be a gilt-edged year that portended huge gains in the stock market and the economy as a whole. Just two days later, the Dow Jones started the plummet that would culminate with it down 45%. This time, the public had little to do with the decline. In the months preceding the extended crash, the US dollar had been devalued, the country was in shock over the Watergate scandal, Bretton Wood systems had slowly collapsed after struggling with bad debt, and the economy was experiencing a recession. At least in this case, the stock market did not stand a chance. The odds stacked against it were too high.

With it, the stock market brought down GDP growth from 7.2% to −2.1% and sent the economy into a spiral of inflation that peaked at 12.3% in 1974. And just like the 1929 Wall Street Crash, the United Kingdom stock market was brought down, too, losing 73% at the same time the American market was hemorrhaging. The UK economy, too, was not spared. GDP growth faltered from a high of 5.1% to −1.1%. The property market also suffered greatly, with the Bank of England being forced to bail out some of the country's lenders. Inflation in Britain continued to rise past the crash to peak at 25% in the year 1975.

Black Monday

As economic globalization swept around the world, stock markets became increasingly interlinked. And with the recent advent of technology use in stock exchanges, brokerage firms were increasingly using automated selling and buying techniques. Because of this, the response to a sustained attack on American warships in the high seas by Iranian silkworm missiles (potential trigger for war) spread alarm across the world. In the closing hours of the Hong Kong Stock Exchange, widespread panic selling caused the exchange to decline in a very short time and start a chain reaction of massive declines in the London, Madrid, Australian, and American stock exchanges.

The Black Monday crash holds the record for the largest decline in the Dow average in a single day (23%). But interestingly enough, even this decline was totally uncalled for. As stated above, the greatest cause for the decline was the fact that automatic sell/buy price triggers were widely in use by investors, which meant that the calming human element of crisis transactions was not in play during this period. After this crash, regulations were put in place to prevent similar panic selling in the form of circuit breakers or trading curbs.

With circuit breakers, trading is halted the moment indices register mass sell orders that could potentially cause massive drops in prices of the whole stock market. Depending on the percentage drop in the index, trading can be closed for one hour to one day. Circuit breakers mitigate against market crashes and reduce the damage in the event that a crash is inevitable.

The Dot-Com Bubble

Also known as the internet bubble, this crash, starting in the millennial year 2000, occurred after almost a decade of oversubscription to the IPOs of tech companies and an accompanying rise in demand for their issued shares that drove prices through the roof. Just like with any bubble, emotions trounced logic as investors overlooked metrics like price-earnings ratio and other technical ratios to continue buying shares of internet companies even when they were overpriced a few times over their real value.

The public joined in the fray of stock trading, with people quitting their jobs to focus their energies on stock trading, fueled by feverish media attention to the huge profits people were making in internet stocks. So wild was the bubble that internet companies could go public with no revenues or real profits. The founders and employees of these dot-com start-ups became instant millionaires. So what if they could not yet access their money because it was locked up by the regulatory SEC restrictions? The prices just kept climbing and climbing—all the more money they would make when they could finally start selling.

In the end, confidence would turn out to be the trigger that caused the bubble to burst. All through the bubble period culminating in December 1999, the interest rates were considerably low as the government anticipated a phenomenon described by pundits as the

Year 2000 problem. However, when no such thing manifested, the Fed announced plans to increase interest rates in February 2000, starting fears of greater volatility in the stock market. However, the bubble continued undaunted, and the NASDAQ-100 Index reached 5,050.

But after a series of downturns, including a failed merger between Yahoo! and eBay, the bankruptcy of Pets.com, and a series of accounting scandals between 2001 and 2002, the stock market corrected and sent the NASDAQ-100 plummeting 78% in October 2002. The dot-com bubble had come and gone and the economy was left smarting from the loss of $5 trillion in total market capitalization. However, the biggest legacy of the dot-com bubble was that it created a glut of office furniture and equipment as offices closed up. Many programmers were also forced to go back to university and acquire the law and accounting degrees they had forfeited to take programming courses and jump into the dot-com bandwagon.

The Stock Market Crash of 2008

The stock market crash of 2008 was the culmination of a decade of misdeeds in the US financial market. Interest rates were maintained at 1% by the Fed starting in 2003, ostensibly to allow the market to recover from the dot-com bubble burst. The low interest rates encouraged massive borrowing, which the real estate market took as an opportunity to encourage massive home purchases. Mortgages were offered at subprime rates, encouraging even more massive borrowing. For the financial markets, a glaring lack of insight caused giants like AIG and Lehman Brothers to overinvest in repackaged subprime loans.

When the real estate bubble burst and borrowers were unable to pay, foreclosures and defaulted payments affected not just the lenders but also the investment banks that had provided them with an endless supply of cash to loan out. AIG was soon in deep trouble, and so were Lehman Brothers and tens of other banks and investment institutions

In the end, the whole sorry situation sent the whole banking industry into a tailspin of failed giants and massive foreclosures. After more than two years of escalation and tensions in the stock market, Lehman Brothers was forced to file for bankruptcy. As one of the oldest traded companies and a perceived sure bet, the companies that no one ever expects to fail, the folding up of Lehman Brothers caused investors to rush the turnstiles as they sought to divest themselves of their stockholdings. Between September 2008 and March 2009, the stock market lost 50% of its value as indicated by the Dow Jones Index.

Chapter 13 Why You Should Invest In Stocks

Ever wondered why Bill Gates still makes it to the top of the Forbes richest every year? Well, rich people have built a system that will generate money for them even while they are sleeping. Their portfolio of investment, in other words, the collection of places where they have invested is done in such a way that they will generate money consistently over a period of time. What can we learn from people who have made money and fortunes that are enormous by any standards?

Income earned from monthly salary is essential to most of the people to sustain their livelihood in the society. We invest so much of our time and energy when we are young to acquire professional skills in order to use them to earn a healthy income. This means our professional knowledge is our main asset that we possess when we join the work force. However, this professional skill is not just our best weapon in the professional world but also that of others; meaning several others who studied along with us or worked with us do own these skills just like us. And this dents our bargaining power in the industry. So, our professional skill is not a mantra that can take us to the paths of riches. Every year thousands of fresh graduates come out of colleges and universities. So, what should you do to stay ahead?

Earning money from paycheck or salary is not a proven way to become rich because it depends on what job you are doing and where you are working. Not everyone is a CEO of a top level company. For those who work as a clerk or technician without any extra perk, it is very difficult to become rich. So, the only way to become rich is by investing money in stocks or shares of companies that are performing well. If you are saving money out of your salary and keeping the money in a savings account, you are not going to get much of an interest on that savings to leap-frog your financial status. But if you have a good savings you can buy shares of companies in a prudent manner and hold on to it till the price rises to a point where you will feel comfortable to sell it off for a good profit. You can even use these shares to get dividends on a long run. In that case, you can earn dividend and then sell the shares in future for a good price. Many people have used this method to pay the college fees of their children or to pay the down payment of their new apartment. The money will always be put to good use if you have a plan in your mind. It will not go waste.

Many people join sales teams and commission agencies to increase their income. Sales agencies work like pyramidal hierarchy system. Once you reach the top of the pyramid hierarchy, you will receive a part of your down level sales commission. This can increase your income but tell me how many people living near your home have made money by ranking high in the pyramidal hierarchy system. Very few and the best examples are fast dwindling. Besides, deviating your focus from your sole income stream and investing your time on sales will lead to losing your job. Many people have fallen victim to this. They did this mistake of investing plenty of time to climb up the pyramidal hierarchy system to earn money at the cost of their day job. Remember what I wrote earlier about rich people; they need not be physically present or even be awake to earn their money. Sales commission cannot be earned without your presence to negotiate with a prospective client and following up with them. Your presence and skills will be tested while negotiating on the price and terms of the deal. On the whole, you are the one who can make the deal happen and "You" need to be physically and mentally present to do sales. None of this is needed to earn money from a stock exchange. You are sitting in front of your desktop or laptop using your own intuition and knowledge to pick up company shares which you deem fit. You may be watching CNN Money or reading the Financial Times while investing in stock exchange. The leisure is all for you to experience.

Now, let us go back a step and see how you should invest money. This is very crucial because if you keep doing what you are doing and still not lose money that is a safer bet than investing it in stocks and losing money. So, let us learn the basics of how to invest and not lose money. Ready for the Gyan?

Chapter 14 Picking Out Stocks to Invest In

Pick a sector that is doing well

When you are picking out stocks, it is important that you find some that come from a business sector that is also doing well. Depending on how the economy is doing, it is possible that some industries will still do well in a downturn, or at least some industries will do better than the rest. There are also times when the economy is doing well, but one or two industries are not doing as well as the rest of the market.

This is why it is so important to pick out industries that are doing well. You may also want to consider spreading your money out a bit so that you can avoid trouble if one of your industries starts to do poorly. And, while it is best to go with industries that are predicted to do well over a long period of time, if you find that one of your industries is not performing the way that you want, it is easy to sell that stock and try something else.

Growing profits

You also need to look for a company that is making profits. If you see a company that is losing money from the start, then it will be hard for you to get a good return on investment. You also want to make sure that the company is getting bigger profits each year. When the company keeps on growing their profits, it is doing well and has a lot of popularity that is growing as well. This makes it a good investment option for many people. The bigger the profits, the better return on investment you will be able to get.

The size of your company

Some investors want to work with a company that is a little bit smaller. They think that these are easier to work with and that they will be able to monitor that company a little bit better than some of the bigger companies. However, there have been some studies done that show how smaller companies will actually carry more risks with them compared to investing in some of the bigger companies.

The reason for this is that a lot of the bigger companies have taken their time to become established. They didn't become big overnight, so you know that they will be safe investments. As a beginner who has never worked in the stock market, it is usually better to go with a company that is bigger and more established. After you have learned how to work in the stock market and you understand the types of risks that you want to take, you can choose to go with a smaller company if you would like.

Also, as a beginner, you should make sure that you are avoiding penny stocks. These sometimes are tempting because they are usually really inexpensive to work with. However, these companies are really risky and often they do not need to provide users and investors with financial information even though they are on the exchange. It is likely that you will lose a lot of money if you choose to work with these penny stocks. It is a better idea to stick with one of the main companies that are on the stock market so that you know they are safer options and you are more likely to make money.

Look at the dividend payments

When you look at a company, check and see if they are able to pay out dividends to their investors. Companies that are able to share their profits already are great options for a beginner to work with. This shows that the company is already able to manage their debts while still sharing the profits with the shareholders. It is likely that they will be able to do it again and you will continue to receive these payments in the future.

Also, when you are deciding how much you can make with dividend payments, you should go with a company that is able to pay you at least two percent. This is a good sign that the company is pretty steady and that you will be able to make a decent amount of money each year. If you can find one that is higher than the two percent, then you are able to make even more in profits.

Manageable debt

While you are taking a look at some of these companies to invest in, you should take a look at the debts that they have. The company doesn't necessarily need to be completely debt free, but they need to have a good balance between the amount of debt that they take on and the amount of profit that they are able to bring out.

There are some good debts that a company will have, especially if they are just starting out or if they have recently undergone an expansion. They may have some debts for their buildings, for their equipment and so much more. You are not likely to find a company that doesn't have any debt, but you should look for one that has kept their debt manageable for the profits that they make each year. If you are looking for a company and they have so much debt that they are barely able to cover it each month, then it is best to go with someone else. In this case, it is unlikely that they will be able to keep managing that debt and you will lose money.

Go with liquid stocks

And finally, another thing that you can consider when you are looking at stocks to invest in is how liquid those stocks are. Liquid stocks are good because these are the ones that you will easily be able to find sellers and buyers for. If you go with a stock that is not liquid, you may find that it is really hard to sell that stock later on when you want to leave the market. Most stocks will have some kind of liquidity with them, but the more liquid the stock is considered, the easier it is for you to sell it when you would like.

Try to find a stock that has a happy medium. You want it to be at a good price, so you do not want the demand for that stock to be too high. If the demand is too high, it will be too expensive to get ahold of it to start. But the demand needs to be high enough that when you are ready to leave the market, no matter what that reason is, you will be able to find someone who is willing to purchase the stocks from you.

There are a lot of things that you will need to consider when it comes to picking out the right stocks for your needs. You should do your research to figure out who is managing the company, how they are doing with their profits and their debts, and find stocks that will be easy to sell if you decide to leave the market. When you are able to do this, you are sure to find some good and secure stocks that will help you to make a good profit.

Chapter 15 Buying Your First Stock

When it the time comes to prepare and make your first trade, you need to consider the how you are going to purchase stocks based on the trading plan you created in the previous chapter. Only by ensuring these things are in order will you be able to get started with the odds in your favor.

Finding a brokerage

The most common way to go about investing in stocks is through a brokerage. As the name implies, a brokerage tasks a broker to deal with sellers and buyers, while at the same time charging a fee for their services and or taking a commission from the profits as well. There are two common types of brokerages, those that offer a variety of additional services, including trading advice and those that are more bare bones in comparison. If you are interested in putting in the minimum amount of work required for a successful return on your investment, then you may be interested in a full-service brokerage that will do most of the work for you. Alternately, you can choose an online brokerage that is little more than a platform for you to do whatever you please.

Unfortunately, comparing brokerages to one another can be more difficult than you might expect, simply because there are so many different ways they can break down their own strengths and weaknesses.

Regardless, you will have to persevere in finding the ideal brokerage for you and this can easily be the difference between success and failure in the long-term. What this means is that you want to pay close attention to the type of fee structure each brokerage employs in order to ensure that your trading approach is enhanced rather than hindered by it. Furthermore, you must also pay special attention to margin rates, word of mouth, commission rates, required balances, and currently active promotions.

Another alternative instead of going through a brokerage is to invest through what is known as a dividend reinvestment plan or DRIP for short. This plan allows shareholders to purchase stock directly from a company, without going through a brokerage at all. In order to get started with these types of plans, you need to purchase shares of a given stock that pays dividends and then reinvest those dividends back into the company in exchange for additional shares.

Research Stocks

Sticking to one type of stock, to start, will make it much easier for you to do the research you need to find the best stocks that are right for your plan. In order to invest in a stock with confidence, it is crucial that you have taken the time to understand exactly what it is that you are getting yourself into. As such, you want to consider the type of company documents outlined below:

10-K

As such, it should naturally be the first thing you look for as it will provide you with a general overview of the company in question. You also want to check out the '10-Q' forms which highlight the specifics of each quarter instead.

Proxy statement

The proxy statement is a type of public statement that provides shareholders with details on proposals, changes in the board of director, along with the compensation breakdown for the leadership of the company.

Annual report

The annual report is different than the 10-k form as it includes the statement from the higher-ups in the company that provide an overall idea of where the company is going in the year ahead, or at least where the top brass is convinced it is going.

Financial statements

For every company that you research you want to look up their balance sheet, income statement, and cash flow statement as together these three will give you a comprehensive financial overview of the company.

Historical Data

While the most recent information on the company is going to be useful, you also want to look into the historical data on the company to determine if where they are at currently was a result of a fluke or if it is the result of years of hard work. This means you would have to take a look at the above documents for the last five years.

Buying your first stock

After you have done your research and found a few stocks that align with your goals as well your plan, it is time to get ready to actually complete your first trade. This can be more complicated than you might expect, however, which is why this section will break down the concepts you will come across when placing your trades. First and foremost, it is important to keep in mind that executing a 'trade' refers to the specific transaction while using the term 'trade' in additional contexts can refer to the type of trading plan or strategy you are using as well.

Depending on the current state of the stock you are considering to purchase, in addition to the direction where the research you have done is pointing you to, not to mention the strength of the market as a whole, you will either want to buy (go long on) or sell (go short on) the stock in question. When placing a trade via a brokerage platform, that trade then goes out via their network and connects you with another individual who is interested in completing your requested transaction. Depending on the type of brokerage you are working with, you may also find they have shares of the requested stock available as well. Either way, just expect to pay fees as well as a commission to the brokerage and make sure that you factor these fees into your trading plan as well.

Regardless of the types of trades you want to complete, you will also be dealing with one or more of the following types of orders:

- Market order

This is a request that you send that sets off the transaction that will result in the buying or selling of a stock. You don't have much control over this request as the market is going to dictate the price you can expect in the transaction.

- Limit order

If, based on your research, you like the look of the direction the stock in question is moving you can set a limit order which says you will buy or sell when the price reaches a certain level specifically. This helps to negate the issue of volatility.

- Stop order

This is the request to sell off all of your shares of a specific stock if the price hits a precise target. This should be set for every trade at a point just above where holding onto the stock becomes unfavorable.

- Stop limit order

This is a combination of the above, and it keeps all aspects of a given stock's movement under close watch for specific triggers.

- Trailing stop order

This is more versatile than a standard stop and will only trigger if the price falls to a specific amount of a preset total as opposed to when it reaches a given price. If you are looking to make truly long-term investments, then these will be your best choice as you can set them based on your overall level of risk assessment.

Chapter 16 Options Trading

In this chapter, we are going to talk more about the details of options. We are also going to learn all of the jargon that is associated with the options markets and learn how to find options to trade.

Call Option

We have already discussed a little bit about what call options are. But let's give a more formal definition. If you opt to purchase a call option, you are essentially purchasing the opportunity to buy 100 shares of the stock at a fixed price. We will see in chapter 5 why people would want to write a call options contract, but that is not really our concern at this point. So, all you need to do is remember that a call option is a specific opportunity for you to purchase 100 shares of stock. Also, the value of call options goes up as share price rises.

Put Option

This option is the opposite of the call option, in that it seeks to profit from a decline in share price. The buyer of a put option has the right to sell 100 shares of stock at the strike price. If the price of shares drops below the strike price, the buyer is at a distinct advantage.

They can buy shares on the option market and then sell them at the higher strike price. The value of put options increases if share price declines.

Exercising an Option

If the buyer of an option exercises their right to buy the shares, we say that they are exercising their right. The seller of the option is then "assigned", that is they are under assignment to sell the shares.

For a put option we say the buyer of the option is exercising their right if they sell the shares to the originator of the contract. Once again, the seller of the option would be assigned.

There are two styles of options. An American style option is one that can be exercised on or before the expiration date of the option. A European style option is one that can only be exercised on the expiration date.

The Main Reason People Write Options Contracts

You can enter into an options contract by logging into your brokerage and selling the options contract to open your position. The reason that you would do this is that you can sell an options contract for a fee which is called the premium. When you sell an options contract to enter a position, you get to keep the premium as profit no matter what happens. In a nutshell, this is the reason why people sell options contracts - to generate monthly income.

There are some risks involved in doing so. If you sell a call contract, the risk is that you are going to have to sell the underlying shares. So, for example, if you own 100 shares of IBM and open a call contract on those shares, the risk is that you will have to sell the shares.

Someone who was using this strategy would probably be hoping that they could profit by selling the options contract to use as a source of monthly income, while keeping the shares. A common strategy is doing it right to be able to sell another options contract the following month. This way you would be able to make some more income from the premium. That works most of the time, but sometimes it is not going to work. If the share price rises above the strike price you selected, you could be assigned and have to sell the shares.

People sell put options for the same reason – to earn monthly income. When you sell a put contract, the risk is that you will have to buy the stock and do so at a high price. So, if someone exercises the contract, you better have access to cash in order to purchase the 100 shares of stock behind the contract.

In most circumstances, the option is never going to be exercised, which is what people are counting on when making put contracts. This way, they basically earn money by selling the put option contract which really is based on nothing. Actually, that is not entirely true. A seller of a put contract is making money on the risk that they are taking by setting up the contract. That is, they assume the risk from someone else. It could be interpreted as someone buying "insurance" on their stock.

Of course, depending on the amount of cash that you need to come up with to purchase stock, the risk could be significant. The real risk is determined by how much the stock has dropped. So at least there is a lower limit to it.

Options Chains (or tables)

These are just lists of options that can be bought or sold. They are grouped by date and then sorted by price. Call and put options are separated or displayed side by side.

Strike Price

One of the most important characteristics of an options contract is called the *strike price*. The strike price is simply the price the shares of stock would be bought or sold for if the option contract was actually exercised. The relationship between the price of the shares on the market and the strike price will determine, in part, the price of the option if it is traded. The strike value is one of the most critical things that you need to look at. When you open up options tables you are going to find that they are listed in order by the strike price for each date. We already saw that when we looked at AMD prices for options on Robin Hood.

When we look at the options for Apple, we see that they are listed in terms of strike price on the left-hand side. You cannot see that below in this screenshot (it is black because it's after hours). The share price is shown at the center of the screen, which is $194.22. The prices on the left-hand side, which denote that the options are calls, are the strike prices.

The price in the box or inside the button on the right-hand side is the price of the actual options contract. You can see that some other information is provided, such as how much the price went up or down today (these look pretty good for Apple, you can see that some gained 30% or more), as well as the percent change needed to get to break even. Break-even is the price that the option must attain in order for you to have no net profit or loss. This will be the strike price plus the price paid for the option for a call, or the strike price minus the price paid for the option for a put.

The strike price of an option never changes. It is set when the options contract is written or sold for the first time. So, if you see an option for Apple that has a strike price of a $193, that strike price remains the same until the option expires, in which case the option no longer exists. So, remember that it is just a fixed quantity, which is a permanent feature of the options contract. Also remember that the strike price and its relationship with the market price is going to be the central factor in determining whether or not the option can be sold at a profit.

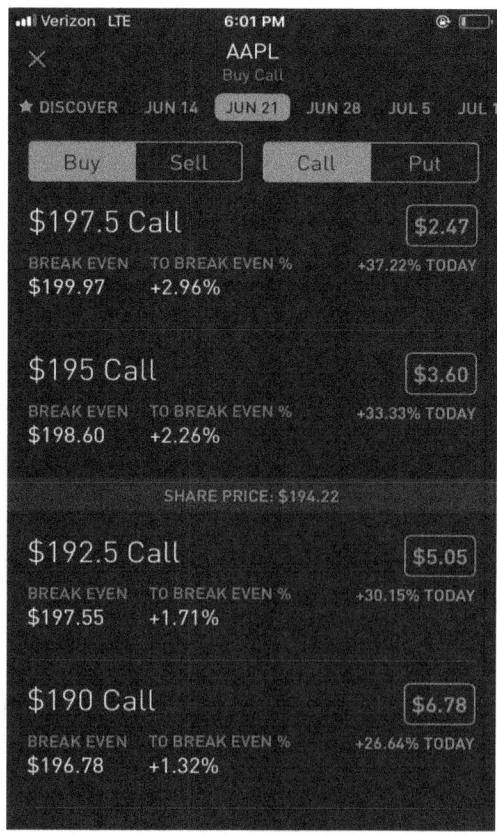

So just to give a specific example, let's look at the option that is right below the line where the share prices are listed. The strike price is $192.50. This means if you owned this option and decided to exercise it, you could purchase the shares of stock at $192.50 a share. That would be true even though the market price or share price of the stock is $194.22.

On the right-hand side, we can see that the quote for the amount of the option is $5.05. This means that you would have to pay $505 to buy one options contract with the strike price of $192.50. The $190 call would cost you $678 to buy.

Expiration Date

The expiration date of the option, just like the strike price, is a fixed quantity as far as the option is concerned. The expiration does not change, and if the option is not exercised on or before the date of its expiration – the option will expire worthless.

Underlying Asset

As per our discussions so far, every options contract has an *underlying*, which is the shares of stock that the options contract controls or represents. So, using the above image as a reference, we listed options contracts for Apple. For each of those, the underlying is 100 shares of Apple stock.

Summarizing main characteristics of options

The main characteristics of the options are the following:

- Call or Put: what type of option is it? If it is a call you have the right to buy 100 shares of the underlying stock at the strike price. All other things being equal, a call option goes up in value if the share price rises. If the price of a stock drops the price of a put option rises (all other things being equal). As you can see, every movement – whether it is upward or downward affects the value of stocks.
- The underlying: this is the asset that backs the option, it is 100 shares of the stock per option contract.
- Strike price: the pre-agreed upon price per share for the stock that underlies the option. If it is a call option, the writer of the contract must sell you the shares at the strike price. If it is a put option, the writer of the contract must purchase the shares at the strike amount.
- Expiration Date: the date the option expires, afterward, it will be worthless and forgotten.

Most Options Expire Worthless

While there is a lot of discussion about the context of options, the vast majority of options contracts, close to 85% on the total, expire worthless. Most options traders are simply hoping to make a profit by buying and selling the options contracts themselves. Even so, if you are going to write options contracts, you do need to be aware that sometimes they do get exercised. In fact, if they expire in the money the broker can exercise them automatically. So, you will need to prepare yourself for that possibility. If you are simply trading options and not writing them, that won't be your concern. There are certain reasons why people would buy options contracts with the hope of buying or selling shares, and we will discuss those. However, most people are not doing options trading for those reasons.

Reading an Options Chain

One of the nice features of newer brokerages like Robin Hood is they make finding an option pretty straightforward. They have basically created an interface that we might call options tables for dummies. However, not all of them are like that, so we should know how to read an option ticker that you find in an options table. Sometimes a listing of options for a given stock like Microsoft, Tesla, or Apple, is called an options chain. An options chain is basically a table listing all the options into sections. One section will include calls, while the other one will include puts.

These are grouped together by expiration date. For example, to find options on Yahoo finance, you can look up a given stock ticker and then click on the options tab. So, let's say that I pull up Microsoft. It will bring up the table shown below.

Calls for June 14, 2019

Contract Name	Last Trade Date	Strike ▲ Last Price	Bid	Ask	Change	% Change	Volume	Open Interest	Implied Volatility
MSFT190614C00090000	2019-06-11 10:46AM EDT	90.00	42.32	42.00	42.15	-1.02	-2.35%	1	2	177.34%
MSFT190614C00100000	2019-06-11 11:24AM EDT	100.00	32.24	32.00	32.10	-0.86	-2.60%	5	314	50.00%
MSFT190614C00105000	2019-06-11 3:25PM EDT	105.00	26.85	27.05	27.15	+0.20	+0.75%	15	18	50.00%
MSFT190614C00107000	2019-06-07 10:48AM EDT	107.00	24.80	25.05	25.20	0.00	-	20	48	95.31%
MSFT190614C00108000	2019-06-07 12:10PM EDT	108.00	23.60	24.00	24.25	0.00	-	44	117	91.41%
MSFT190614C00110000	2019-06-11 1:40PM EDT	110.00	21.45	22.05	22.25	-1.95	-8.33%	20	47	92.19%
MSFT190614C00112000	2019-06-11 3:15PM EDT	112.00	19.80	20.05	20.20	-1.85	-8.55%	20	82	76.56%
MSFT190614C00113000	2019-06-11 12:24PM EDT	113.00	18.75	19.05	19.25	-1.90	-9.20%	12	23	80.08%
MSFT190614C00114000	2019-06-10 2:32PM EDT	114.00	19.15	18.05	18.10	0.00	-	19	53	50.00%
MSFT190614C00115000	2019-06-11 10:24AM EDT	115.00	18.15	17.05	17.25	+0.50	+2.83%	11	387	72.27%
MSFT190614C00116000	2019-06-06 3:55PM EDT	116.00	11.70	15.95	16.45	0.00	-	46	57	76.17%
MSFT190614C00117000	2019-06-07 12:03PM EDT	117.00	14.55	14.95	15.30	0.00	-	1	125	58.59%
MSFT190614C00118000	2019-06-10 2:03PM EDT	118.00	15.25	14.05	14.30	0.00	-	11	80	64.45%
MSFT190614C00119000	2019-06-11 3:09PM EDT	119.00	12.85	13.05	13.20	+1.10	+9.36%	1	226	51.17%

As you can see at the top and it tells us the expiration date for the options. Several bits of information are listed from left to right; like stocks, options have their own tickers. These are shown in the far-left column. Each ticker contains valuable information. If you can read the tickers you can basically know what you need to know about the option. Let's take one as an example. We will use the bottom one in the table, which is this one.

MSFT190614C00119000

Obviously, the leading string of characters is the stock ticker for the underlying stock, in this case it is Microsoft. Next, we see a string of numbers which ends right before the C. So, firstly you have the two-digit identification of the year, which in this case is 2019. You need to know the year because there are some options that expire one and two years into the future. Secondly, you have the two-digit identification of the month, which in the example shown here is 06, namely June. The next two digits identify the day of the expiration. In this case, it is 14, so what this tells us is that the option expires on June 14, 2019.

If you see a ticker for an option, you definitely want to pay attention to the letter in the middle. In this case, it is a C, which tells us that this is a call option. If there was a P there, that would mean it was a put option. The last part of the string gives you the strike price of the option. It gives three places for the decimal so, although it says:

119000

what that means is really $119. Remember that the strike price is not the price of the option, which is the price that would be paid per-share if the option were exercised. In this case, the writer of the contract would be required to sell you the shares at $119 per share if the option was exercised.

So, the options ticker provides us with information about the permanent characteristics of the option, or what tells us the underlying, the expiration date, the type of option and strike value. It also has a lot of changing characteristics that we have to read from the table by moving across it left to right. This may be a bit confusing as you are at the first stages of learning, however, with a lot of exposure, you will be able to work through all this data in a breeze soon enough.

Furthermore, if you look at the first column, this shows you the last time the option was traded. Next, we see the strike price: in our example, it is $119. Next to the strike price, we see the most recent price that was used for trading the option. So, this is basically its current value. Here it says $12.85. Remember that there are 100 shares underlined in the option. Therefore, the price for this option is $1285.

Next, we see two columns to the right with more prices. The first one is the *bid*, and the second one is the *ask*. Bid and ask tell you the values that people are willing to pay or accept for the sale of this option. In checking the bid for our example, we can see that the price is $13.05. That tells you that traders are *offering* $13.05 for the option. Again, that is a per-share quote, so the actual price is $1305.

Ask is the current asking price that traders, who are trying to sell the option, are trying to get. In this case, it is $13.20, which is quite a bit more than the bid - so it might take them a while to actually close a sale. If you owned this option, and wanted to sell it quickly, you could sell it for the price at $13.05 or below. If you go with the ask price, you might have to wait.

Next, the table tells you how much the price of the option changed during the day, and then this is followed by the price change in percentage terms. So, this option gained $1.10 for the day, which was an increase of 9.36%.

Volume tells you the number of contracts that were bought or sold that trading day. So, in this case, there is only one contract. That is not a very interesting option since it is not trading very much.

Moving to the right, the next column is open interest. That tells you how many contracts there are in reality, that have not been exercised: these are active positions. In this case, the number listed is 226. So, there are 226 options contracts with this strike price and expiration date that have not been exercised.

The final column is *implied volatility*, and it gets quoted as a percentage. Implied volatility tells you the expected volatility of the stock between the present date and the expiration of the options contract. If the option price is increasing the implied volatility will be large. So, looking at the table, consider the option with the strike price of $90. The implied volatility for that one is 177.34%. On the other hand, looking at the option with the strike price of $119 is much closer to share price, while implied volatility is lower at 51.17%. That is actually fairly high as well.

If you are not familiar with volatility, it is simply defined by how rapidly and by how much the price of the stock changes over time. So, a stock which is changing a lot every single day has high volatility. In contrast, an older stock that is more stable, say like Walgreens, is going to have lower volatility. You can visualize volatility by imagining that a smooth straight line is of low volatility, while one over the same time period that zigzags a lot and goes up and down a lot, is one with high volatility.

All other things being equal, an option with high implied volatility is going to be priced higher than the same option with low implied volatility. You want higher implied volatility when trading options. If you check beta on the stock market, you can get an idea of how volatile the stock itself is. A beta larger than 1 is a more volatile stock.

What you really want to keep in mind with implied volatility, is that for a given option, it is going to be affected to variations in the underlying price than one with lower implied volatility.

The Broker

To trade options, you will need to open a brokerage account. This is no different than doing so in order to invest in stocks. You will need some basic information like a bank account, and some brokers might require an ID or proof of address. But it is usually pretty quick and easy. Robinhood is a great broker to use for trading options if you are a beginner, so consider downloading their mobile app.

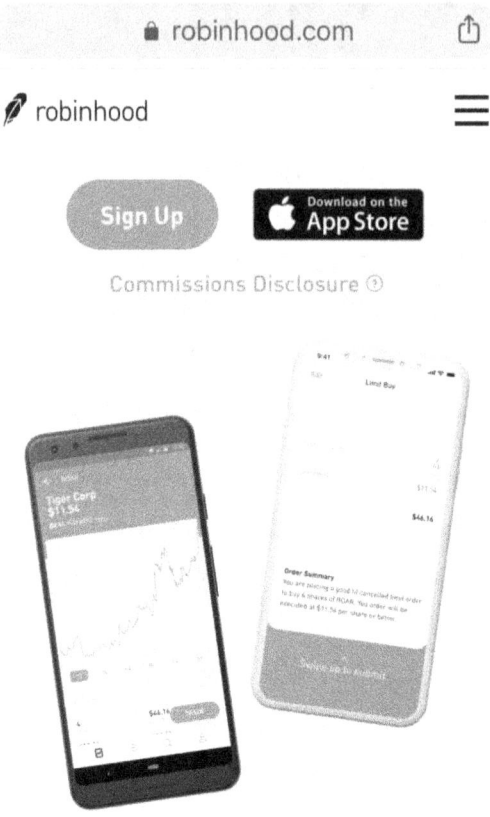

If you already have a broker, consider using them for trading options. In fact, you are going to use the same broker that you use for stocks in most cases. Mainly what the broker does is facilitate the buying and selling of shares, and in this case they will buy and sell options on your behalf.

If you have a large account, the broker may be willing to lend you money to buy and sell shares or options, in which case you would have a margin account. You are required to deposit $2,000 to open one. Since commissions can eat into profits from options trades, it is important to look for a broker that has low or no commission fees. We have already talked about Robinhood, which does not charge commissions. Besides Robinhood, a good brokerage option to consider is *Tastyworks*. They are focused on trading options and they have low commissions and fees.

Besides any commissions, you will want to know whether or not a given brokerage has a minimum amount of money you need to deposit in your account in order to open trades, and what that minimum is.

The Market Maker

Market makers play a fundamental role behind the scenes when it comes to options trading, and also in other financial markets. These are large players with financial institutions or brokerages that ensure the markets run smoothly.

The truth is you really do not need to know much about the market maker because they operate behind the scenes. What the market maker does, is use their accounts to facilitate trades when there is no actual trader available to buy or sell a contract. They also maintain their own large portfolio.

So, if there was a certain options contract that you wanted to purchase, but there was nobody selling one, in order to keep the market running smoothly the market maker could sell that options contract to you out of their portfolio. The stated goal of a market maker is to ensure that a given market, which in this case is the options market, has sufficient liquidity. This enables traders to buy and sell their positions quickly, meaning you don't have to wait around for a buyer to materialize over an extended time period when you need to get out of a position.

Instead, you could sell your position to the market maker immediately. So, in short, the market maker is a large financial institution that will by contracts to put in their portfolio when there is no willing buyer in the market, or they will sell contracts when there is no willing seller in the market. This all happens behind the scenes, for this reason you are not going to know who or what is actually executing the transaction.

Market makers are people that are contracted to trade on the markets for this purpose. They may work for a financial institution or a brokerage firm. They have to use their own capital in order to participate in the transactions. Market makers have to be very experienced traders in addition to having access to enough capital to take care of the transactions.

Chapter 17 Swing Trading Strategies

To see success with swing trading, you need to make sure that you are working on the right strategy. There are a lot of different strategies that you can work with when you are ready to join the market, and each of them has potential to earn you a profit if you properly use them. But you have to know how each of them will work and you need to stick with that strategy throughout your whole-time trading.

Learn from Your Mistakes Instead of Being Discouraged by Them

If everybody makes mistakes, why should you think you're an exemption and beat yourself up over them? Successful swing traders remain unperturbed by losing trades but instead, they persist wisely by learning from their mistakes.

Find and Stick to Trading Strategies That Work for You

While starting with the most popular trading strategies is a good place to start swing trading, you must come evaluate the results you get from your chosen strategy to see if it's worth continuing, tweaking or replacing.

What do you need to consider when evaluating whether a trading strategy is something that you should stick to, tweak, or ditch? One is risk appetite. If your risk appetite is on the low side, maybe you shouldn't even be trading at all. If it's moderate, your trading strategy must be one that carries a moderate amount of risk, too.

Plan Your Swing Trades

Many traders make the mistake of just following the herd with nary a clue of why they're adopting the strategies of the trading herd and what the risk-reward tradeoffs of such strategies.

Looking at good patterns

One thing that you can look at is the charts for a particular stock you would like to look through. There are a lot of different patterns that can come up all the time and the way that they look will determine whether they are a good one to use for your trade or if you should go with another option. When you notice these patterns, you will be better able to predict how the stocks that you want to work with will behave in the future and use this to make a profit.

Ditch the Micro Time Frames

With swing trading, you must focus more on the longer time frames because they're less volatile and by doing so, you minimize your risks for "false triggers" or whiplashes that can make you take positions on securities whose prices are still on a decline. The shortest time frame you should consider is daily, nothing less. The longer your time frame, the lesser the false triggers and noise you'll encounter, and the more you can maintain your winning swing trading streak.

Trend Following

No matter what strategy you decide to use, you will need to make sure that you understand how to read charts and trend lines.

Even though the current price is the most important price, you will want to pay attention to all of the prices that you see for every day that you take into your analysis.

Managing Your Money

One of the biggest tips to help you figure out how much money to put towards a stock is by evaluating the risks associated with the stock. You will be able to do this through any strategy that you will use and various other factors that are part of your trading plan.

Follow the Rules and Guidelines

One of the biggest reasons you need to make sure that you are following your guidelines is because the more consistent you are with your trading, the more likely you are to become successful. Furthermore, you will want to make sure that you follow the guidelines as they will help you to think systematically when it comes to making decisions.

Diversity

Diversity is one of the more popular controversies when it comes to trading. While some traders feel you need to have great diversity, which is a variety of stocks, in your portfolio others feel that this isn't as important. In reality, the more serious you want to be with your trading, the more you will focus on diversity. However, this isn't always true when it comes to investors. But, as stated before, investing and trading are two different career paths in the stock market.

Always Note the Risk

Another important factor to pay attention to when you are looking into trend following is how much risk is involved if you decide to take on the financial instrument you are looking at. When you are looking at the risk, you always have to pay attention to your guidelines and your trading plan.

Using Options as a Strategy

Options are known to be a great strategy if you are looking for leverage, which is when you increase a return on a trade through borrowed money. It is important that you need to make sure you will only use this strategy if it will help you to receive more of a profit. In fact, this is one of the most important factors of choosing a strategy. You have to make sure that it is going to help you gain a profit and decrease your risks.

Short Interest

This is a great strategy to learn as a swing trader because it can show when the stock market is about to go into bearish conditions, which means that the stock prices will start to go down. Furthermore, short interest can also warn you about short squeezing.

Pay Attention to the Float

However, this is also the trick when it comes to the float strategy. There tends to be a fine line between having a massive float and having a float that will give you the best profits. The reason why a massive float, which would be too many shares, can cause you to lose capital instead of increasing your profits is because if you have a huge float, the price won't move as quickly. However, if you have a smaller amount of shares in your float, then you will find that the price moves a bit higher, of course this gives you a larger profit. With this said, you also don't want to have too little shares in your float. If this happens, then you won't be able to make much of a profit either as this can stop your float from increasing in price.

Breakout and Breakdown Strategies

When you focus on the breakout strategy, you are looking at the history of your stock's trend line in a microscopic fashion. When you are looking at the trend line, you will see every time the price has gone up and down. Stock prices are almost constantly changing throughout the day, which is what the trend line shows.

Every now and then, you will notice in the trend line that you have a several high points and several low points. These high points indicated the highest prices of the stock and the lowest points show the lowest prices.

The biggest difference between the breakout strategy compared to the breakdown strategy is the condition of the market. If you notice that the stock has been going on an upward trend for a while, you will use the breakout strategy. However, if you notice that the trend shows the price has been decreasing over time, you will use the breakdown strategy.

News Playing

As you know by now, one of the most important parts of your day is your pre-trading portion. This is one of the first things you will do once you start your day. You will want to do this before you start trading; however, you will probably be checking out the stock market so you can see the changes in your stocks and any target stocks that you are watching.

However, one of the most important parts of this part of the day is reading the news that happened over night. This is important because you need to know what news is going to affect what stock, especially if you own the stock. You should always make note that any type of news can affect the pricing of financial instruments. For example, if you read that a company donated a large amount of money towards a nonprofit organization, people might be more likely to invest in that stock. However, if you read any negative news about a company, you will find the stock price going down because people are selling their shares.

Be Flexible

While you want to follow the rules and guidelines, you should also remain flexible. First, you want to remember that life happens. Sometimes we plan to sit down to work but we have to go pick up a sick child from school or have a family emergency. When this happens, we might not be able to complete the financial instruments that we took on. This means that you will either keep them in your portfolio and take any loss or hope for a gain or you can trade them and close out for the day. When you are flexible, you will realize that this situation will be fine, and you won't dwell on the fact that you couldn't complete the job as you should have.

Remaining flexible will also help when you find yourself with unrealistic expectations, which is a common mistake among traders. On top of this, it will help you realize that mistakes happen and you shouldn't put too much emphasis on them.

Remember the Research

Learning is a common theme as a trader. It doesn't matter what type of trading you find yourself taking on, you will always want to make sure that you learn as much as you can before you start your career and continue to learn. There are a variety of ways that you can focus on research and learning with swing trading.

Join an Online Community

Another great way to learn about swing trading and meet other traders is to join an online community. There are several websites that are comprised of forums run by some of the most experienced swing traders today. These forums are extremely beneficial to any trader for a variety of reasons. First, beginners can go join the community and receive more tips, trading lessons, and other information that will help them become successful. Second, this is often a location where beginners meet their trading mentor. Third, this is a place where traders can go to not only get the most up-to-date information on the profession but also get to know people who are like them. It is always important to feel that you are not alone, especially when find yourself struggling with a part of trading. There will be hundreds, if not thousands, of people who will be interested in helping you.

Pick a strategy that is easy

Some beginners think that complex strategies are the best to increase their profits. But these complex strategies can be really confusing and overwhelming for someone who is just beginning. Go with a simple strategy, at least until you learn more about the market.

Start in one place

Many beginner traders will start out by trying out too many markets at once. This can make it hard to know what you are doing. Stick with one market and one pattern and concentrate on that for now.

Don't forget a stop loss

This is one of the main reasons that a trader will lose all their money. They will forget the stop loss and not watch the market enough, resulting in a huge loss in the process. Always use stop orders to help you reduce your risk.

Look at market indicators

These market indicators can help you to determine which way your trading will go and are not things that you should avoid looking through.

Chapter 18 Forex Strategies and Strategies for Beginners

Forex Trading strategy is what forex traders do to buy or sell financial instruments at a given time to generate profits. Forex Trading strategies are nowadays done, either manually or automatically. A trader is using manual strategies when he or she interprets the trading signals and as a result, decides to buy or sell.

Before choosing a Forex Trading strategy, it is important to identify which of these four trading styles fits your personality:

1. Day Trading

Day trading is a short-term trading style designed to buy and sell financial securities within the same trading day. That is closing all positions by the end of the trading day. In Day Trading, you can hold your trades for minutes or even hours. Day traders deal with financial instruments like options, stock, currencies, and contracts for difference. Many day traders are investment firms and banks. Day traders use technical analysis to make trading decisions.

Pros

- Day traders are not affected by unmanageable risks and negative price gaps because all positions are closed by the end of the trading day.
- There are a substantial number of trading opportunities
- Traders can be extremely profitable due to the rapid returns

Cons

- Traders can be extremely unprofitable due to the rapid returns
- You don't have to be concerned with the economy or long-term trends
- Huge opportunity cost
- Day traders have to exit a losing position very quickly, to prevent a greater loss.

2. Swing Trading

Swing trading is where a trader holds an asset between one and several days in an attempt to capture gains in the financial market. This type of traders doesn't monitor the screens all day, and they do it a few hours a day. Swing traders usually rely on technical analysis to look for trading opportunities. Swing trading position is held longer than day trading position but shorter than buy and hold investments. They have larger profit targets than day traders.

Pros

- Swing traders can rely solely on technical analysis, which simplifies the process
- Requires less time to trade compared to day-trading

Cons

- Swing traders are exposed to overnight and weekend risks
- Generally, swing trading risks are as a result of market speculation
- It is difficult to know when to enter and exit a trade when swing trading

3. Scalping Trading

Scalping is the fastest trading style where traders hold positions for a very short time frame. Traders here gain profits due to small price changes. The scalpers hold a position for a short period to gain profits. Traders with large amounts of capital or bid-offers spread narrowly prefer scalping.

Scalping follows four principles:
- Small moves are more frequent - even when the market is quiet, scalpers can make hundreds or thousands of trades
- Small moves are easier to obtain - small moves happen all the time compared to large ones
- Less risky than larger moves - scalpers only hold positions for short periods therefore because they have less exposure the risk is also lower
- Spreads can be both bonuses and costs. Spread is the numerical difference between the bid and ask prices. Various parties and different strategies view spread as either trading bonuses or costs.

Pros

- Positions can be liquidated quickly, usually within minutes or seconds
- Very profitable when used as a primary strategy
- It's a low-risk strategy
- Scalpers are not exposed to overnight risks

Cons

- Requires an exit strategy especially during large losses

- Not the best strategy for beginners; it involves quick decision-making abilities.

4. Position Trading

Position trading involves holding a position open for a long period expecting it to appreciate. Traders here can hold positions for weeks, months, or even years. Position traders are not concerned with short-term fluctuations; they are keener on long-term views that affect their positions. Position trading is not done actively. Most traders place an average of 10 trades a year.

This strategy seeks to capture full gains of long-term trading, which would result in an appreciation of their investment capital. Position traders use fundamental analysis, technical analysis, or a combination of both to make trading decisions. To succeed position, traders need plans in place to control risk as well as identify the entry and exit levels.

Pros

- Traders have a longer period to reap fruits.
- Trader's time is not on demand. Once the trade has been initiated, all they can do is wait for the desired outcome

Cons

- Traders may fall victim to opportunity costs because capital is usually tied up for longer periods.

- Position traders tend to ignore minor fluctuations, which can turn to trend reversals, a change in the price direction of a position.

Forex Trading Strategies

There are several types of forex strategies; however, it is important to choose the right one based preferred trading style to trade successfully. Some strategies work on short-term trades as well as long-term trades. The type of Forex strategies you choose depends on a few factors like:

- Entry points - traders need to determine the appropriate time to enter the market
- Exit point-trader need to develop rules on when to exit the market as well as how to get out of a losing position
- Time availability

If you have a full-time job, then you cannot use day trading or scalping styles

- Personal choices

People who prefer lower winning rates but larger gains should go for position trading while those who prefer higher winning rate but smaller gains can choose the swing trading

Common Forex Trading strategies include:

1. Range trading strategy

Range trading is one of the many viable trading strategies. This strategy is where a trader identifies the support and resistance levels and buys at the support level and sells at the resistance level. This strategy works when there is a lack of market direction or the absence of a trend. Range trading strategies can be broken down into three steps:

- Finding the Range

Finding the range uses the support and resistance zones. The support zone is the buying price of the security while the resistance zone price is the selling price of a security. A breakout happens in the event that the price goes beyond the trading range, whereas a breakdown occurs in the event that the price goes below the trading range.

- Time Your Entry

Traders use a variety of indicators like price action and volume to enter and exit the trading range. They can also use oscillators like CCI, RSI, and stochastics to time their entry. The oscillators track prices using mathematical calculations. Then the traders wait for the prices to reach the support or resistance zones. They often strike when the momentum turns price in the opposing direction.

- Managing Risk

The last step is risk management. When the level of support or resistance breaks, traders will want to exit any range-based positions. They can either use a stop loss above the previous high or invert the process with a stop below the current low.

Pros

- There are ranges that can last even for years producing multiple winning trades.

Cons

- Long-lasting ranges are not easy to come by, and when they do, every range trader wants to use it.
- Not all ranges are worth trading

2. Trend Trading Strategy

Another popular and common Forex Trading strategy is the trend trading strategy. This strategy attempts to make profits by analyzing trends. The process involves identifying an upward or downward trend in a currency price movement and choosing trade entry and exit points based on the currency price within the trend.

Trend traders use these four common indicators to evaluate trends; moving averages, relative strength index (RSI), On-Balance-Volume (OBV), and Moving Average Convergence Divergence (MACD). These indicators provide trend trade signals, warn of reversals, and simplify price information. A trader can combine several indicators to trade.

Pros

- Offers a better risk to reward
- Can be used across any markets

Cons

- Learning to trade on indicators can be challenging.

3. Pairs Trade

This is a neutral trading strategy, which allows pair traders to gain profits in any market conditions. This strategy uses two key strategies:

- Convergence trading - this strategy focuses on two historically correlated securities, where the trader buys one asset forward and sells a similar asset forward for a higher price anticipating that prices will become equal. Profits are made when the underperforming position gains value, and the outperforming position's price deflates
- Statistical trading - this is a short-term strategy that uses the mean reversion models involving broadly diversified Security Portfolios. This strategy uses data mining and statistical methods.

Pros

- If pair trades go as expected investors can make profits

Cons

- This strategy relies on a high statistical correlation between two securities, which can be a challenge.

- Pairs trade relies a lot on historical trends, which do not depict future trends accurately.

4. Price Action Trading

This Forex Trading strategy involves analyzing the historical prices of securities to come up with a trading strategy. Price action trading can be used in short, medium, and long periods. The most commonly used price action indicator is the price bar, which shows detailed information like high and low-price levels during a specific period. However, most traders use more than one strategy to recognize trading patterns, stop-losses, and entry, and exit levels. Technical analysis tools also help price action traders make decisions.

Pros

- No two traders will interpret certain price action the same way

Cons

- Past price history cannot predict future prices accurately

5. Carry Trade Strategy

Carry trade strategy involves borrowing a low-interest currency to buy a currency that has a high rate; the goal is to make a profit with the interest rate difference. For example, one can buy currency pairs like the Japanese yen (low interest) and the Australian dollar (high interest) because the interest rate spreads are very high. Initially, carry trade was used as a one-way trade that moved upwards without reversals, but

carry traders soon discovered that everything went downhill once the trade collapsed.
With the carry trade strategy:

1. You need to first identify which currencies offer high rates and which ones have low rates.
2. Then match two currencies with a high-interest differential
3. Check whether the pair has been in an upward tendency favoring the higher-interest rate currency

Pros

- The strategy works in a low volatility environment.
- Suitable for a long-term strategy
- *Cons*
- Currency rates can change anytime
- Ricky because they are highly leveraged
- Used by many traders therefore overcrowded

6. Momentum Trading

This strategy involves buying and selling assets according to the strength of recent price trends. The basis for this strategy is that an asset price that is moving strongly in a given direction will continue to move in the same direction until the trend loses strength. When assets reach a higher price, they tend to attract many investors and traders who push the

market price even higher. This continues until large pools of sellers enter the market and force the asset price down.Momentum traders identify how strong trends are in a given direction. They open positions to take advantage of the expected price change and close positions when the prices go down.
There are two kinds of momentum:

- Relative momentum - different securities within the same class are compared against each other, and then traders and investors buy strong performing ones and sell the weak ones.
- Absolute momentum - an asset's price is compared against its previous performance.

Pros

- Traders can capitalize on volatile market trends
- Traders can gain high profit over a short period
- This strategy can take advantage of changes in stock prices caused by emotional investors.

Cons

- A momentum investor is always at a risk of timing a buy incorrectly.
- This strategy works best in a bull market; therefore, it is market sensitive
- This strategy is time-intensive; investors need to keep monitoring the market daily.

- Prices can shift in a different direction anytime

7. Pivot Points

This strategy determines resistance and support levels using the average of the previous trading sessions, which predict the next prices. They take the average of the high, low, and closing prices. A pivot point is a price level used to indicate market movements. Bullish sentiment occurs when one trades above the pivot point while bearish sentiment occurs when one trades below the pivot point.

Pros

- Traders can use the levels to plan out their trading in advance because prices remain the same throughout the day
- Works well with other strategies

Cons

- Some traders do not find pivot points useful
- There is no guarantee that price will stop or reverse at the levels created on the chart

8. Fundamental Analysis

This strategy involves analyzing the economic, social, and political forces that may affect the supply and demand of an asset. Usually, people use supply and demand to gauge which direction the price is headed to. The Fundamental analysis strategy then analyzes any factors that may affect supply and demand. By assessing these factors, traders can determine markets with a good economy and those with a bad one.

Forex Strategies for Beginners

When starting on Forex Trading, it important to keep things simple. As a beginner, avoid thinking about money too much and focus on one or two strategies at a time. The following three strategies are easy to understand and perfect for beginners.

1. Inside Bar Trading Strategy

This highly effective strategy is a two-bar price action strategy with an inside bar and a prior/mother bar. The inside bar is usually smaller and within the high and low range of the prior bar. There are many variations of the inside bar, but what remains constant is that the prior bar always fully engulfs the inside bar. Although very profitable, the inside bar setup does not occur often.

There are two main ways you can trade using inside bars:

- As a continuation move - This is the easiest way to trade inside bars. The inside bars are traded in trending markets following the direction of the trend.
- As a reversal pattern - the inside bars are traded counter-trend

When using this strategy, it is important to look for these characteristics when evaluating the pattern:

- Time frame matters - avoid any time frame less than the daily.
- Focus on the breakout - best inside bar trades happen after a break of consolidation where the preceding trend is set to resume.
- The trend Is your friend - trading with the trend is the only way to trade an inside bar
- A favorable risk to reward ratio is needed when trading an inside bar
- The size of the inside bar in comparison to the prior bar is extremely important

2. Pin Bar Trading Strategy

This strategy is highly recommended for beginners because it is easy to learn due to a better visual representation of price action on a chart. It is one of the easiest strategies to trade. Pin bars show a reversal in the market and, therefore, can be useful in predicting the direction of the price. Pin bars consist of one price bar, known as a candlestick price bar, which represents a sharp reversal and rejection of price. Candlestick charts are the clearest at showing price action.

There are various ways traders trading with pin bars can enter the market:

- At the current market price
- Using an on-stop entry
- At limit entry, which is at the 50% retrace of the pin bar

To improve your odds when using the pin bar strategy:

- Trade with the trend
- Wait for a break of structure
- Trade from an area of value

Some of the mistakes pin bar traders should avoid include the following:

- Assuming the market will reverse because of a pin bar
- Focus too much on the pin bars and miss out on other trading opportunities
- All pin bars are not the same and should not be treated as such

3. Forex Breakout Strategy

A breakout strategy is where investors find stocks that have built strong support or resistance level, wait for a breakout, and enter the market when momentum is in their favor. This strategy is important because it can offer expansions in volatility, major price moves, and limited risk. A breakout occurs when the price moves beyond the support or resistance level. The breakout strategy is good for beginners because they can catch every trend in the market. Breakouts occur in all types of market environments.

Traders establish a bullish position when prices are set to close above a resistance level and a bearish position when prices close below a support level. Sometimes traders can be caught on a false breakout, and the only way to determine if it is a false breakout is to wait for confirmation. False breakout prices usually go beyond the support and resistance level; however, they return to a prior trading range by the end of the day.

Good investors plan how they will exit the markets before establishing a position. With breakouts, there are two exit plans:

- Where to exit with profit-traders can assess the stock recent behaviors to determine reasonable objectives. When traders meet their goals, they can exit the position. They can either raise a stop-loss to lock in profits or exit a portion of the position to let the rest run
- Where to exit with a loss - breakout trading show traders clearly when a trade has failed, and therefore they can determine where to set stop-loss order. Traders can use the old support or resistance level to close a losing trade

Pros

- You can catch every trend in the market
- ·Prices can quickly move in your favor

Cons

- Traders can get caught in a false breakout
- It can be difficult to enter a trade

Tips for trading breakouts:

- Never sell on breakdown or buy on breakout both carry extreme risks

- Trade with the trend
- Wait for higher volume to confirm a breakout
- Take advantage of volatility cycles
- Enter on the retest of support or resistance
- Have a predetermined exit plan

Note

Beginners are more likely to be successful in trade than their experienced counterparts are because they have not yet cultivated any bad habits. Experienced traders have to break bad habits and put aside any emotions built over the years.

Chapter 19 Setting your Financial Goal

After dealing with your debts and saving for an emergency fund, the next step is to plan what you will use your money for. Allocation of resources is one of the most basic problems that the study of economics tries to deal with. This problem exists because we have a limited amount of resources and an endless list of needs and wants.

The key to solving this problem on a personal level is to identify the needs and wants that you want to prioritize the most. You may do this by looking into the different options where you can spend your money on and identify the ones that you really want to work for. Let's start with the first step:

Step 1: Identifying Future Goals and Expenses

Setting a solid financial goal starts with your ideas. You may start by thinking of the things that you want to buy in the future. Most of us are already doing this. However, only a few actually do more than think about their dreams. Instead, most people only do wishful thinking and hope that one day they will have enough money to achieve their goals.

To start your own goal setting process, make a list of the things that you want to buy in the future. Some of the things that you may have in your list may be really important like buying a home or setting up a retirement fund. Others, like taking a big vacation or buying a sports car are not as important but they may make us happier.

After creating your list, put a number beside each item with the number 1 assigned to the most important goal. Here is a sample list that you can base your own on:

1. *Create a Wedding Fund*
2. *Buy a home that's big enough for the family*
3. *Save for kids' college fund*
4. *Save for dream travel destination*

Some goals have a predetermined deadline. If you have kids for example and you are saving for their college fund, the fund needs to be ready by the time they graduate from high school.

Step 2: Setting a Target Amount

When working for your financial goals, you need to deal with them one at a time. While we want to achieve all the goals in our list, we are more likely to accomplish goals faster when we focus our financial resources on the ones that are most important to us. When that particular goal is done, we could move on the next task on our list.

Step 3: Planning the Saving Timeline

Now that you have your financial goals set, pick the most important one and set the timeline for saving for that goal. By plotting the timeline, you will be able to know how long you have to save for the goal.

Pick a financial goal that is still a couple of years away from completion and set it as the target of your stock investing activities.

Step 4: Assess the amount of growth you need to reach your goals

The general idea behind investing is that you will need to make your savings grow so that you will reach your financial goals faster. You want to set the right expectations when it comes to the growth potential of your investments. Some of your trades will yield north of 15% while others will end up with losses. It is more realistic to expect a modest rate of return of 7% to 10% each year. Some beginners who make early mistakes in the stock market may experience even lower rates of return on their first few years of trading. While these rates of return may seem low, they are still better than many of the investment opportunities out there.

Knowing the average rate of return in the market, you will be able to make assumption on how long it will take for your funds to grow to reach your target amount. If you have $10,000 right now and you invest it and get an average of 8% rate of return per year, it will take you more than 9 years to reach a $20,000 target. You can increase the rate of reaching that target by adding more capital to your fund each month. You may also increase the rate of growth by taking high growth rate stocks in the beginning of the trading period.

To learn the relationship of the rate of return to the amount of time it takes you to reach your goal, use a compounding interest calculator. In this type of calculator, you will need to enter the capital amount, the number of years that you will be investing, and the annual rate of return you are expecting to get the final amount. Any additional income you earn in the market will be reinvested to it to create a compounding effect. This will help you reach your target amount faster.

Step 5: Practice with Paper Trading

If you find that the stock market is the best place to invest for your financial goals, you can increase your chances of success by practicing your trades. You can start practicing by doing trades on paper.

You can start a paper trade by taking a notebook and taking notes of the stocks that you want to invest in. You could then start by choosing one of these stocks and do a mock trade. In your mock trade, you pick the stock; you also identify your buying price and the volume of your purchase. Lastly, you set the conditions where in you will sell the stock. In the following days, months or years, you could then start to track the stock that you picked to assess the performance of your mock trade.

You could make the mock trade even more realistic by creating a budget that is similar to the budget that you will have when you actually start trading. This will prevent you from being reckless in your stock picks.

Mock trades like this allow you to practice with your trading strategies. If your mock trades often end up with losses, you may need to make changes in your trading strategy.

Paper trades also allow you to become more familiar with the market and the different events that are going on in the moment before you even participate in the market. It allows you to experience how it would be like to invest in the companies that you consider to be within your circle of competence.

The key to paper trading is to do it as many times as you can. This will allow you to know which indices, sectors and companies are most profitable.

Step 6: Get Started

Now that you know what you want to achieve and what you need to achieve it, start working on your financial goals. You can begin by saving for your investment capital. Ask your broker for the minimum amount that you will need to start investing. While you are saving, start studying the companies that you will buy with your initial investment amount. This will ensure that you will be ready to start investing when you have saved the minimum investing amount needed.

Chapter 20 Technical Analysis

At the core of every successful investor is a number-crunching geek who understands stats and the way they can be used to determine the value of a stock. Also, these stats can be used to identify the patterns and trends that a stock may have.

As you become more and more familiar with the various tools available to you, you will be able to recognize the floors, ceilings, resistance levels, and other measures that go along with trading stocks and other financial instruments.

That is why we will focus on developing a better understanding of the various types of measures out there. Also, it should be pointed out that this information may or may not be available for free. Often, analytical data packages and other statistical information may be available by subscription only or as part of a full-service broker's platform. This is especially true of real-time data. So, it certainly pays to look into what such a service may cost you and if the cost is worthwhile to you.

That being said, let's move on to the various technical analysis tools available to investors.

Patterns and Trends

Investors will quickly come to recognize charts depicting the price of an asset and how these prices may indicate a pattern or a trend. For instance, a monthly chart for the price of an asset may reveal a downward trend, that is, the actual lines on the chart mark a trend in which the price of the asset is going down. Similarly, the trend may be for the price of the asset going up.

In these cases, you may identify that price fluctuations are an outlier, and you can either sell at an unusually high point or buy at an usually low point. Either way, you can pick up on these trends the longer you observe the price of an asset.

Also, certain patterns may emerge, such as the breakout pattern. This pattern can be seen when the price of an asset may be ready to take off, especially after a long period in which it remained within a specific trading range or has been unable to break a specific ceiling.

For example, a stock has been trading in an $18-$20 range. The resistance level seems to be $20.However, you begin to observe a "W" pattern as the price goes up, and then down, then up, and then down, and then up. The stock might be poised to take off each time it hits the floor ($10). You might expect that, each time the stock rebounds, it may break the resistance level at its ceiling. While this may not be entirely predictable, you can make a rather educated guess in this regard.

By the same token, you might be looking at a reversal, that is, a stock which looks to be gaining momentum but actually seems poised for a downturn. This is when a stock's chart shows an "M" pattern: down, then up, then down, then up, and then down. The concern with this pattern is that the stock may break it resistance level and fall further down than the previous floor.

As you begin to detect these types of trends and patterns, you will gain a better understanding of when to get in and when to get out.

Moving Average

The moving average is the average price of a stock calculated at a given interval. Generally, it is measured at hourly intervals. As such, the moving average is a good indicator of a stock price's trend.

The most common measure for a moving average is the two-day moving average. This measure allows an investor to see if the trend of the stock is upward or downward, depending on what the data reflects. Ultimately, an investor may contrast the two-day, 10-day, 50-day and 200-day moving averages to see where the trends lie.

For example, if the two-day average is lower than the 200-day moving average, then you might be in for a reversal. Consequently, if the two-day average is higher than the 200-day average, then you might be poised for a breakout. So, it certainly pays to keep an eye out for the moving average of any given stock.

Candlesticks

These tools are similar to the moving average in that they may be tracked on an hourly basis. However, the difference with candlesticks is that they measure the high price and low price of an asset at each interval.

When charted, the high and low price form a box. The box will be larger the further apart the low and high prices are. The box will be shorter the closer both prices are. When boxes are big, they are considered "bullish", as the asset price may be testing a resistance level. However, if the boxes are small, then they may be considered "bearish", as the asset price is trading within a tight range.

Also, a trend line may be derived from the candlesticks. Therefore, the trend line may reinforce the bullish and bearish designations. The most important thing to keep in mind when looking at candlesticks is that they reflect the range in which a stock is being traded. Therefore, the investor must be on the lookout for the floors and ceilings which may be emerging. As the floors and ceilings gain strength, the investor may be able to determine when to buy and when to sell, based on the candlesticks.

On-balance Volume

This is a tool which measures the supply and demand of a given stock.

For instance, if the volume is increasing, it means that the supply of a stock is healthy. It means that investors are willing to sell. This is the usual trend when the price of a stock is rising or already high. Therefore, investors want to sell, in order to make profits.

This trend also is an indicator that investors are willing to push the price up higher and higher. Of course, it's important to take resistance levels into account, as stocks may hit a ceiling and then come tumbling back down.

Conversely, when on-balance volume indicates that there is low supply, then it is a sign that investors feel the price is low. Thus, investors might be waiting for the price to rebound. In fact, this trend may be a good indicator to buy, as the price of the stock is low.

By the same token, the price of the stock may have encountered a resistance level at the bottom. Therefore, investors might be willing to test a lower floor.

Divergence
In the event that the on-balance volume and price were going in different directions, then the presence of divergence may become evident. So, you might have increasing supply with a price trending downward. This might be an indicator that a breakout is set to happen. By the same token, the on-balance volume may be falling, while the price of the asset may be trending upward. This type of divergence may indicate the possibility of a reversal.

As you can see, divergence is a very useful pattern to keep an eye out for. Since price is all about supply and demand, be on the lookout when supply and demand are contradicted by price, as it may indicate that a breakout or reversal is about to take place.

Experience

As you become familiar with the type of assets you are trading, you will recognize which prices and trends are normal. As such, you will be able to identify outliers by simply looking at the lines in a simple plotting of the asset's price.

This is due partly to technical knowledge and partly to experience. As you gain experience, you will become more and more confident in your own judgment. Now, this is not to say that you won't need technical tools, but rather your experience will help you determine if the numbers you are seeing are indicative of where the trend is going.

Often, you will hear experts contradict numbers or offer their explanation as to why the numbers don't reflect reality. It could simply be that a given price point may be unjustified and is due to irrational behaviors on the part of investors.

Other times, it could be that overall uncertainly and market volatility may send investors looking for safe haven investments. For instance, high levels of volatility in the stock market may lead investors to flock to the bond market. Therefore, the unusual dips in the price of certain stocks may not be consistent with your experience.

In addition, your experience also may help you to identify resistance levels. So, when you see an asset's price falling to a certain point, you might be able to identify a given floor. By the same token, you might be looking at a specific ceiling which you feel is a threshold that the asset's price may or may not break.

Then, there is a plain, old gut feeling about things. You might get a gut feeling that something is not right, as the number don't really add up. In this case, you might be inclined to divest and move on to another asset. By the same token, you feel that something is about to happen, as the numbers don't really paint such a bad picture. In this case, you might choose to invest in that asset.

So, your experience will certainly come in handy the longer you stay in the business.

Chapter 21 Fundamental Analysis Strategy

Now, it's time to get into some of the information that you need to know in order to pick the right kind of investment strategy. Going into the stock market without some kind of strategy can be dangerous. You will have no idea of the best stocks to choose, when to enter the market, or any other information that will lead you to making smart decisions with your investment.

The first strategy that we will take a look at for investing in the stock market is fundamental analysis. This is a pretty straightforward idea when it comes to investing in the stock market, but it will require research, patience, and time. The goal of this kind of analysis is to look over any company you want to invest in, and then figure out what its intrinsic value is.

Basically, the intrinsic value of a company is how much it is worth compared to the price it is currently being traded at on the market. If you do some research about the company and find that the intrinsic value is higher than the current market price of the company's stocks, then this is a good investment, and you should make a purchase. In this scenario, the trader believes that the stock is going to go up in time, and purchasing the stock at this low price can be a good way to save money and increase profits.

There are a few different methods that can be used when it comes to finding the intrinsic value of a company, but the ideas behind all of them are pretty similar. You will spend your time trying to figure out how much the company is worth. This will usually be the sum of its discounted cash flows. This basically means that the company is going to be worth all of its future profits when they are added together, and this number is going to be discounted to account for time value. Time value is the force of which the $1 you receive today will be worth less in the future.

The idea behind the intrinsic value of a company equaling its future profits can make sense when you think about how a business is supposed to provide some value for the owners. If you are a small business owner, the worth that you get from that company is all of the money that you can take home at the end of the year. And you can only take something home if you have a little left after paying for supplies, debts, salaries, and anything else that is necessary to keep the business going. A business is always about the profits or any revenue it makes minus the expenses. Once you can figure this out, you will have the intrinsic value of a company.

In order to come up with the numbers that you want with this, you just need to do a little bit of research. Having a good look at the financial report of the company and checking out some of the news about them and the numbers that come around with this company. But with a bit of research, you will find that you can figure out the intrinsic value and pick the right companies.

The biggest part of doing a fundamental analysis is going to be delving into a lot of financial statements. It will look at all of the financial aspects of a company, including its liabilities, assets, expenses, and revenue. The reason that this information is explored is that it gives the analyst insight on how the company is going to perform in the future.

When we are talking about stocks, the fundamental analysis is going to help determine the value of security by focusing on any of the underlying factors that can affect the actual business dealings of the company, as well as taking a look at its prospects. It is also possible to do fundamental analysis of the economy or on certain industries as well, but we are just going to focus our attention on individual stocks for this time.

The fundamental analysis is going to answer several questions such as:

- Is the revenue of that company growing or not?
- Is the company actually making any profits?
- Is the company in a position that is strong enough to beat out its competitors, both now and in the future?
- How well is the company able to repay the debts that it takes out?
- Is the management following all the rules or is there some trouble with them trying to cook the books along the way?

Of course, these questions are very involved, and there are other questions that you may want to ask about as well. It is basically going to all come down to just one question: is the company's stock really a good investment? The fundamental analysis, when it is done properly, will be able to help you answer this question before you decide to invest.

One thing to note here is that the term fundamental analysis is often going to be used when it comes to stocks and purchasing them. However, it is fine to do this kind of analysis on any kind of security. As long as you take the time to look at the economic fundamentals, then you are basically working with a fundamental analysis. We will continue to keep our focus on doing a fundamental analysis with stocks for this time.

Quantitative vs. Qualitative Fundamentals

The different fundamental factors that you can work with can be grouped into two major categories known as qualitative and quantitative factors. The financial meaning of these terms isn't really different compared to their regular definitions, but the best way to describe them is as follows:

Quantitative: This is anything that can be measured or otherwise expressed in numerical terms.

Qualitative: This is based on the quality or character of something, rather than being based on the quantity or size of something.

For the terms of this guidebook, we will use quantitative fundamentals as numeric or measurable characteristics of a business. It is easy to understand how most of the quantitative data for a business will be found in its financial statements. It is simple to figure out the assets, the profit, and the revenue by some simple measurements.

You can also work with the qualitative fundamentals. These are often going to be less tangible actors that surround a business, things that could include the quality of the members on the board, the recognition of the brand name, the patients, or more for that business.

Neither of these two methods is necessarily better than the other. In fact, many investors will choose to do a combination of the two to help them get the best information before they invest in one stock over another. Being able to look at some of the stuff that goes on in a business, and checking that they are actually able to bring in a profit as well can be so important to ensure you see some results from your analysis.

Is the Fundamental Analysis the Right One for Me?

There are a lot of great benefits to going with the fundamental analysis. It allows you to see how the company is doing and then compares that information to how you think the company will do in the future. For investors who are looking for a way in order to get in the market and find some good deals, the fundamental analysis is the right tool for you.

As we will see in the next chapter, there are some individuals who like the idea of technical analysis instead. These traders find that, while there may be some exceptions, most companies are valued where they are on the market because of some reason. They don't believe there is such a worry as undervaluation or overvaluation of a company, and so working with fundamental analysis wouldn't make sense. These individuals focus more on picking out stocks based on charts and figures rather than on the intrinsic value of a company.

With that said, the fundamental analysis can still be a great one to work with. It allows you to be able to find some great deals on stocks, ones that you may not have even looked at in the past. Many of these companies may be overlooked with other strategies simply because they are valued at a lower mark and may not have reached their full potential yet.

Working with fundamental analysis is a great way to help you find some good stocks to work with. You will need to spend some time looking at the intrinsic value of a stock and figure out if there is some reason that it is maybe being undervalued on the market. Once you can find this information, picking out the stocks that will work for you, and investing in them before the price movement catches on and goes up, will be easy and you will be able to make a good profit from that trade.

Chapter 22 Cutting Your Losses

It is an easy and well-understood expression to "cut your losses." The advice can save many an investor from losing their shirt on a potentially failing stock. But ironically, it seems like very few tend to savor that advice. New investors are often caught up in the decision to HODL or cut their losses. They're not sure if the stock is going to rally or just wither away from the stresses of the market.

No investor deliberately chooses a stock they believe is going to lose its value to the point that it is worth less than it did when they bought it. It stands to reason that if you're investing in the stock market, you are expecting to increase the value of your portfolio.

Your objective is not to eliminate losses but to reduce your exposure to them as much as possible. So, if you've invested in a stock and it suddenly takes a downward turn, you're faced with an important decision. Your ability to know when to ride the wave of recovery or cut your losses will make the difference between an amateur investor and success.

Why People HODL

First, it helps to understand why people choose to hold on even when all hope is lost. It serves as a reminder that the stock market is pure mob psychology at work. Often, even in the face of clear signs to the contrary that the stock is not going to recover, they still hold on. Then, when all is lost, they fail to realize that their loss was not the result of bad timing or poor research, but instead, it was their own behavior that was the trigger. There are several reasons why this happens:

- *Unfailing loyalty:* As you look at your charts, almost every stock will show a zigzag line that starts in the lower left quadrant and gradually rises to the upper right. Given enough time, most stocks will go up in price even in the worst of times. The hope that the stock will eventually bounce back and make an astronomical recovery is in the heart of all people. The fact that some stocks have made such a move gives them even more hope. So, even if there is a huge drop in value, they will continue to hold on tightly, waiting for recovery. Sadly though, many stocks that lose value drastically may never fully recover and regain their former highs.

- *Pride:* Sometimes, it's just pride that gets in the way. Unwilling to admit that they made a mistake can compel them to hold on, proving their point that they were right all along. They will say things like, "it's not a loss until I sell it," they continue to stubbornly hold on to their position.

- *Neglect:* When stocks are performing well, it is easy to log on to your account and watch the money grow, but when they begin to show losses, that same exercise can be painful. Even if only a few stocks are failing, it can bring down the returns for your whole portfolio and you get the feeling that the whole bag is not worth your interest anymore. They turn off their computers like they are turning away from the scene of an accident rather than going in and just getting rid of the bad apples. The losses continue to grow unseen until the entire portfolio grows completely out of control.

These and many more reasons are at the heart of capital losses for new investors. Making the decision to hold on is not usually based on any type of real logic and sadly, it can lead to disastrous results. It pays to know when it is best to cut your losses and move on to more promising ventures than to continue to hold on in spite of evidence to the contrary.

Realizing Your Losses

While getting into the market is the key to investment riches, it is just as important to know when it is your cue to leave. It is inevitable when investing in anything that you're not going to get it right 100% of the time. Even the most successful investors have experienced huge losses, how much more for the new investor just getting into the market.

Once you accept this fact, then you can realize how important it is to have an escape clause in your investment plan. The sooner you are able to realize your losses, the better protection you can implement for the rest of your portfolio.

Imagine that you are invested in ten different stocks and indexes. After a short while, you notice that three of your stocks are starting to erode and you're beginning to bleed money. But the other seventeen stocks are still doing well so you assume that it will balance out in the end. The problem with this thinking is that the longer the losers stay in play, the more of your profits from the other stocks will be eaten up. So, for every gain you make from your good decisions, you are losing a significant percentage to those stocks that are eating away at it. It would be much better to shed those bad apples earlier, so you can protect those gains that are doing well for you.

Stop-Loss Protection Strategies

Here are a few strategies you can try to protect your gains:

- 3 to 1: For every gain, you receive, cut your losses at a 3 to 1 ratio. So, if you are making gains at 25%, then you should cut your losses at 8%, which is 1/3 of the profits.

- Recognize when you're wrong: When the price of the stock drops below what you paid for it, chances are you've made a mistake. If the stock continues to decline, don't wait around in hopes of recovery. For each point it continues to drop, your losses are growing. You can figure out what you did wrong later. For now, it's time to cut and run.

- Recognize the loss when it happens. Some are of the belief that loss occurs only when you sell it but in reality, if your portfolio has lost its value, you've already suffered a loss.

Remember, all stocks carry a risk of loss. It takes courage to close the door and leave some of your hard-earned money behind. But, the sooner you learn to cut those losses and move on, the better for your portfolio and your future earnings.

Chapter 23 Taking Your Profits

It is a lot easier to sit back and watch your money roll in when you've made a good decision. But even in the area of profits, there are those investors that make mistakes. In order to take your profit, you must have a time when you are going to let go of your stock. The question is when. Some investors see the price inching its way up the charts and declare they will bail at the point when the stock reaches its peak. The problem with that thinking is that it is not always easy to recognize this point and they end up waiting too long.

Ideally, the best time to unload a stock is when everyone else wants to buy it. Even if you could predict the peak point and try to sell, chances are you'll be unloading it at a time when it is on the decline and you'll have fewer buyers looking to buy in. But, if you decide to sell when the stock is still very strong, and the price is still climbing, you'll have a much easier time of it, and you'll avoid getting caught in that endless cycle of corrections that comes after a stock reaches the top.

Have a Plan

When it comes to knowing when to take your profits, you need to have a plan. As a matter of fact, having a profit plan is just as important as choosing the right stock. Over time, you will develop your own set of guidelines for buying and selling but that does not mean you can't start with a plan from the very beginning.

Talk to any investor today and they'll happily give you their own personal guidelines that have worked for them. There is no perfect strategy to know when to sell and reap your rewards but as you grow in your knowledge and experience, you will quickly learn what works for your portfolio and what doesn't. Here are a few key points that will help you develop your own personal plan of action.

- Successful stocks, once they move out of their base on the charts, will move up as much as 20-25% before they start their decline. Deciding to sell at that 25% pivot point would save you from having to take losses when the price starts its natural decline.

- If the price rises quickly – sell quickly, don't wait for the 25% peak.

- Cut your losses at 8%.

- Reevaluate the stock after you take your profits to decide if you want to reinvest for long-term profit.

- Sell stocks that are slow earners and put the money into proven winners.

As you gain more experience, you will be able to compound your profits simply by knowing when to take your profits and run and when to reinvest.

When to Sell

There are two important points to keep in mind when it comes to selling your stocks.

- If you choose right, then your selling is easy.

- Avoid big-sell off periods.

When you see stocks sold in huge numbers, it may be the knee-jerk reaction of an emotional investor base. Always check your charts to see if big sell-offs are common for that stock so you don't get sucked into a trap. Winning stocks may have pullbacks from time to time, but they rarely drop below 8% unless you bought at too high a price.

There are a few telltale signs to look for when it comes to selling stocks and taking your profits.

- Get out at the first sign of trouble while your stocks have still earned you a profit.

- Look for the largest daily price run-up. If a stock has had a significant run from its base, and the close for that day is larger than on any other day, it usually means it is near its peak. It's time to sell.

- Look for the heaviest daily volume. As the stock is reaching its peak, the volume will increase. Usually on the day with the heaviest volume, it will be at or near the top.

- Look for the gap. If a stock opens with a large gap in price from the previous day after a run-up, this is referred to as an exhaustion gap. It's a sign that it is peaking.

- Climax top activity. If a stock's rise to the top is so fast and active, and it continues the activity for several weeks (a climax top), it means that there is heavy volume distribution with no real price benefits.

- Distribution signs. When there is an increase in daily volume but no increase in price, sell.

- Stock splits. If a stock has a run-up of 25-50% in just a few weeks after a stock split, sell.

- When there are more consecutive down days.

- Check the 200-day moving average. Stocks can be sold when they are 70-100% above the 200-day moving average.

- On the way down. By all means, if the stock price is declining, don't wait for a rally. Lock in your profits and sell to cut your losses.

- When you see a new high with low volume.

- When the stock begins to close near the low for the day.

- If you see an attempt at a rally but it is ineffective.

No matter what level of experience you have, it is extremely important that you learn as you go. While it is very important for you to do research and prepare when to buy a stock, it is just as important to do a post-mortem after you sell. You want to know what you could have done differently, how to rake in more profits, and what mistakes to avoid the next time.

When to HODL

There are times when it is okay to stay in the market and ride it out. If for example, you choose to buy strong growth stocks, and you have developed a price target based on your research and earnings expectations for several years, then you will want to hold onto those until it reaches your target price.

This strategy follows the buy low and sell high concept. Still, there are a few steps that you'll want to have in between to make sure you're not holding onto a dud.

- Watch the stock's performance for a few weeks to make sure that it is behaving as you would expect.

- Follow the market closely and make sure it's following the general market movements.

- Chart a cutoff point on a graph showing the point where you will sell if it starts to lose money - a sell line.

- If it stops rising, do not let it fall back down to the original purchase price.

The reality is that you can't win if you don't play, and you can't play if you're not willing to lose. Still, you can cut your losses exponentially if you have a plan to reap your earnings whenever you can. Even if you expect a stock to rally, it is better to pull out in cash, wait for the rally to confirm, and then reinvest when it is more stable.

So, whether you are losing in the market, gaining profit or HODLing, it is very important that you follow the guidelines and have a concrete plan moving forward. These are the things that turn you into a savvy investor that will earn you the profits you've been looking for.

Chapter 24 Managing your Money

In this chapter, we're going to be looking at how to manage your money, especially via external structures. We'll talk about things like Money Managers, Financial Advisors, and Mutual Funds. We'll examine if you need them, and how to decide to choose them.

Let's get started, shall we?

As we stated at the beginning of this book, the material in this book was written for people with little to no professional or corporate financial management knowledge who want to invest in the Stock Market, and in the previous chapters, we've examined many of the basics that you will need to know to start to play in the world of stocks and investments. But then, the question arises, should you hire a professional financial adviser to help you in the management of your portfolio and your investment?

First off, it's important to mention that many people now realize that they cannot solely depend on a financial advisor to manage their portfolios. The crashing of stocks and other markets in recent years has established the need for anyone who is investing in any market to do some form of research and ensure that they gain knowledge in that area. In other words, whether you end up hiring a financial adviser or not, you cannot afford to slack off in learning about the stock market, as well as doing research on any stock that you buy. After all, it makes no sense to trust someone else with your money when you have no idea what they are planning to do with it.

Choosing or Using a Financial Advisor

A financial advisor is someone that helps you manage your money. They help you manage how you invest, save, and spend money. A financial advisor usually offers a wide range of services on everything that has to do with money. Now, the level of influence and interaction that the financial advisor has with your funds is up to you and the structure between both parties, that is, you and the advisor. The term financial advisor covers a wide range of services, ranging from investment planning, financial consulting and certified financial planners. There are also digital financial management options such as robo-advisors, where you are not necessarily interacting with a human manager. But more on this later.

What can a Financial Advisor do for you?

A financial advisor is an *expert* in financial matters, who provides various services hinged upon managing money, investments, and savings. Therein lies the core of financial advising. The influence of technology has made it possible for ordinary people to enter into the financial market without going through the formal training necessarily. That said, certain kinds of knowledge are available to only those who are formally trained financially and can access and take advantage of. In other words, the fact that you can access the stock market, in some form at least, and make trades does not mean that you know everything that there is to know about the market. This is where a financial advisor comes in.

A financial advisor can, among many other things, help you assess your financial situation, set or review your financial goals, and help you chart a path to achieve those goals. So, a financial advisor will examine your assets, expenses, and debts, and then help you identify how exactly you can improve. They can also help you work to reduce spending, figure out insurance and tax, increase your savings, and invest your money. Since a financial advisor has professional expertise and experience, they can help you improve your portfolio significantly. A good financial advisor can be of help when it comes to achieving your goals of financial independence and freedom.

Types of Financial Advisors

There are quite several types of financial advisors, both in terms of services offered and the contexts in which the services are provided.

Let's take a look at some of these financial advisors:

CFP: A CFP or Certified Financial Planner helps you do just that, plan your finances. A CFP must be licensed by a professional board in your country, such as the Certified Financial Planning Board of Standards in the U.S. To become a CFP, they must be educated thoroughly, pass through a rigorous test and demonstrate some level of work experience. These kinds of financial advisors are primarily aimed at helping you create goals, actionable goals for your finances that you should follow to achieve your goal as you go on.

Broker/Stockbroker: This kind of financial advisor assists you with investments and explains how to invest your money. A stockbroker buys or sells financial products (i.e., stocks) for their customers and typically receives a fee for doing this. To become a broker, you must be licensed by the U.S Security and Exchanges Commission in the US or any other equivalent board in any country where you may be based.

A Registered Investment Advisor: This kind of advisor gives advice and recommendations to investors for certain. RIAs are usually registered with the Security and Exchange Commission, or some other form of investor, depending on how large or small the company is. Some of these Investment advisors tend to focus on investment portfolios, while others seem to take on a more general and holistic view.

Also, it is not uncommon for a particular individual or company to offer the services of more than just one specific discipline. The reason for this is that it is not very realistic for an average person to employ a CFP only to plan their finances, and simultaneously employ another broker to manage financial instruments and other investments solely. Many individual financial advisors are licensed to act in multiple offices, or the company that they work for offers these services as part of a particular package.

How much does it cost to hire a Financial Advisor?

Perhaps you are already thinking; if a financial advisor is this good, or can offer this level of services, then I should probably patronize them; well, pump your brakes first. You need to consider the cost implications of hiring a financial advisor. Many advisors charge different types of fees and at different rates, but here are some of the more common ones.

Hourly Rates: Some advisors charge between £75 per hour to about £350 per hour. In the UK, for example, the rates tend to hover around £150.

Set Fees: Some Financial advisors also request a fixed fee for performing a specific piece of work. It could range from a couple hundred to even a thousand dollars.

Monthly Fees: This option is usually reserved for those who are planning to use the advisor or their company's services for a long time. The advisor and the client can work out a specific fee that will be paid monthly for as long as you utilize their services. The fee could also be a portion of the money that you were seeking to invest.

Manage an Ongoing Fee: This scenario is closely related to that of paying a monthly fee for a service that is ongoing.

These are some of the combinations of fees that can be charged by financial advisors, and as you can see, they are quite expensive. Imagine that you have to pay a monthly service fee or a percentage of your investment money for the rest of your life, and it becomes costly. It is for this reason that many people are skeptical about using a Financial Advisor.

Should You Use a Financial Advisor?

The choice of whether to use a financial advisor, in the form of a broker, a CFP, or an Investment Advisor, is more of a personal one, rather than a general one. In other words, you have to look at your personal circumstances and see if it fits with your budget, time, and personal investment strategy.

One of the things that you need to consider is the kind of investments that you are making and how risky they are. Generally, the more risk you are willing to take on, the more you should be willing to use the services of a financial advisor. For example, if you are investing in mutual funds, there is little, if any, need for a financial advisor. However, if you are looking to enter the stock market to purchase individual stocks, then the risks you are taking on are more significant, and you might want to employ the services of a professional to assist you in managing the portfolio.

Another point to consider is the size of your portfolio. The larger your portfolio is, the more likely it is that you will need professional advice. Plus, a broader portfolio account can easily absorb the fees associated with hiring a financial advisor.

Finally, you should take out time to do your research before using a financial advisor. One of the best ways to get a financial advisor is to ask people around you who have enjoyed success in the stock market over a consistent period. While past profits are not a guarantee of future earnings, it is easier to trust someone that has a record of being somewhat successful than someone who hasn't had much success in the market.

If possible, try to create a list of as many advisors that you'd like to speak to, and schedule a conversation with them. You should do that offline, by the way. While online interviews and conversations are good starters, you should not decide to trust a person or company with your hard-earned money without at least meeting them. When you meet, ask questions about their investment strategy, whose trading style and philosophy they subscribe to, and how they plan to manage your portfolio. Most of the time, the first consultation is free, as it allows you to get to know each other without the pressure of finances forcing you to perform. The other thing is, as this is free, you have the choice to meet several and choose one whose mentality suits yours.

When you meet, ensure that you do not leave the meeting with any doubts about what you're getting into. Do not allow yourself to be bamboozled with high-sounding and complex language that you do not understand. I mean, you must insist that every term that you do not understand is explained, and every service charge is explained. Of course, you must be fair in your dealings too. Your advisor is a professional and deserves to be paid well for their expertise and sometimes experience.

Digital Alternatives to Financial Advisors

In recent times, more brokerage companies have been implementing digital investment management solutions. Two of these new developments are robo-advisors and Online Financial Planning services.

A robo-advisor is a digital service that offers simplified and low-cost investment management. To make use of it, you answer a few questions on the brokerage company's website, and then complex algorithms help you build an investment portfolio according to the goals that you have set and the risk appetite that you have indicated that you are comfortable with. In this way, robo-advisors help monitor and balance your investment, ensuring that your portfolio is managed correctly. What's more, a robo-advisor costs a fraction of what a real-life human financial advisor will cost.

Another option is online financial planning services. This is much closer to traditional advisors than a robo-advisor. The online service gives you access to human financial advisors who can help you manage your investments, among other things. Some packages grant access to the type of automated investments that you'll get from a robo-advisor, as well as the ability to consult with a team of financial advisors. Some more expensive alternatives grant you access to the kind of one-on-one service that you will have received from a traditional offline advisor.

Surprisingly, both of these options are relatively cheap, as well as being flexible. Some companies even charge a large percentage of their fees from the profits that they help you make. Before you select a financial advisor, especially online, ensure that you understand everything that they are offering, possibly speak to their support teams to gain an understanding of what exactly you will be charged.

Mutual Funds

A mutual fund is a financial vehicle that is made up of a pool of money that has been collected from many investors. A professional money manager manages the portfolio of a mutual fund. They collate the assets of the funds and invest it in a diversified portfolio to produce gains for the investors. The objective of a mutual fund is to generate income for the investors, and as such, the portfolio is structured and maintained to match the goals of the investment, as stated in the mutual funds' prospectus.

Investing in a mutual fund gives individual investors such as yourself access to a professionally managed and diversified portfolio of bonds, equities, stocks, and other securities. Every shareholder will gain and lose proportionally to the gain and losses that the funds make. Mutual funds tend to invest in a large number of securities, and the overall performance of the fund is tracked as a change in the market capitalization of the fund, which is an aggregated performance of the individual investments in the portfolio.

Understanding Mutual Funds in Depth

A mutual fund works by aggregating money from multiple investors to build an extensive portfolio, and then invest that money in various types of assets. These include bonds, securities, and equities. Thus, the overall value of the mutual fund depends on how each security or assets that are bought perform. So, in purchasing a unit of a mutual fund, you are buying into the mutual funds' performance or, better still, a part of the portfolio's value. You have invested your money into buying a fraction of many types of assets - a condition that you could not have carried were you to invest on your own. This is what makes a mutual fund different from other types of stock investments. The fact that a share in a mutual fund represents a share in many different stocks and other assets.

It is for this reason that the price of a share of a mutual fund is called the Net Asset Value (NAV) per share, or sometimes referred to as the NAPS. A mutual fund's NAV is found by dividing the total value of all the securities it holds by the total number of outstanding shares. Outstanding shares are the shares held by all institutional investors, shareholders, insiders, and company officers. Also, the value of a mutual fund's share can be bought or redeemed at the current NAV, which remains stable, unlike the price of a stock. The NAV of a mutual fund does not fluctuate but is settled at the end of each trading day.

Income is earned from a mutual fund in 3 major ways:

- Interest is earned on the dividends in stocks and interests on bonds held in the portfolio of the funds. Generally, a fund pays out a majority of the funds that it receives in a single year to investors in the form of a distribution. Usually, there is an option for investors to either receive a check or reinvest the earnings to get more shares.

- If the fund sells assets that have appreciated, then the fund is said to have a capital gain. Most funds also transfer these gains to the investors during a distribution at the end of a financial year.

- If the holdings of the fund appreciate but are not sold by the manager of the funds, the value of the fund shares increase in price and then you can sell your mutual fund shares on the open market.

Should you invest in a mutual fund?

Why should you consider investing in a mutual fund? Well, for starters, mutual funds help eliminate or at least reduce risk. As we have said in a previous chapter, diversification is essential to keep your risks low. Or put in simple language, you shouldn't put all your eggs in one basket. Consider an investor that invests in Apple or Amazon stocks. Now, if the buy came just before the company had a lousy quarter, then the investor would lose a great deal of money because all his investment is tied to that particular company.

On the other hand, if the investor had used that money to buy shares in a mutual fund, then the loss will be mitigated. That is because the mutual fund has stocks in other companies; the loss will count for a little part of the fund's portfolio. In this way, a mutual fund helps you avoid any significant losses, but at the same time, you don't get any big wins either.

Imagine the flip-side of our analogy, where Amazon or Apple had a great quarter and outperformed the competition. Any investor that invested solely in that company would have made a lot of money. On the other hand, an investor in a mutual fund with a stake in a company will not make as much profit, because that company's stocks are only a part of the fund's portfolio. It's a classic risk and reward scenario: the higher your risk, the higher your chances of reward and vice versa.

It is important to say that if you are already investing in a retirement package, then you are most likely investing in some sort of mutual fund. In this case, you can decide to go for a riskier alternative. You might decide to invest directly in the stocks of a company.

So, as a recap, let us re-examine what we've looked at in this chapter. While you can invest in the stock market on your own, sometimes, it may make sense to look at hiring the services of a professional financial advisor. However, the fees charged by many traditional professional advisors are quite high and can hurt your portfolio, especially if it isn't large. A good alternative is a robo-advisor or an online financial planning system. These digital platforms provide financial services similar to a traditional financial advisor but usually at a much cheaper rate. They take into consideration your present financial situation as well as your goals and help you plan how to achieve them. Lastly, you can invest in a mutual fund if you are seeking a way to diversify your investment and reduce risk. However, you should know that your profit might tend to be on the low end. Remember, once again, high risk, high reward, and low risk, low reward.

Chapter 25 Diversification

Investing in the stock market involves more than just putting your money into an account and watching it grow. There are a lot of decisions to be made. You not only have to decide what you want to invest in, how much to invest, and where to invest. You also have to decide on HOW you will invest.

One of the biggest decisions you will need to make is on how you will diversify your portfolio. Any investor worth his salt knows how important it is to diversify. This is a rule that not only applies to the stock market but in a variety of areas of life. You don't study only one subject in school, you don't buy at only one market in your community, and you don't date just one individual before you settle down.

The old saying, "Don't put all your eggs in one basket," is a very valuable lesson for everyone to learn.

In the stock market, it is one of the most important rules you can apply. Those who are only interested in one or two stocks may fare well, but when those stocks begin to backslide, they can easily take their money with them.

On the other hand, if you research one or two stocks very well and you can gauge the market correctly, you can do quite well with just those investments. Other investors may have their hand in twenty, thirty different options and because they have so many, will not research any of them well and may suffer losses because of it.

So, the question before now is simple: How much should you diversify? It is clear that diversifying can work as an insurance policy, but too much diversification can cripple your returns. You don't want your portfolio to be too large, nor do you want it to be so small that you are vulnerable to the natural fluctuations of the market.

A basic guideline to remember is the more you diversify, the less skill and knowledge you have to apply to your investment strategy. Ideally, to get the maximum results possible, you need to focus on the areas you know well and have the time and ability to follow.

So, what is the magic number? Again, that is for each person to decide but many experts suggest you have only one or two big profit winners and a few smaller options in your portfolio. If you plan on having a large portfolio, then choose four or five of those stocks in industries that you understand. If, by chance, another great opportunity was to present itself, have enough discipline to sell something you already have and replace it with the new stock.

Exercising this guideline can help you leave emotion out of the trade. Because you will have to give up something that is already proving profitable, it will impel you to take great care in researching a newer prospect before impulsively just jumping in. This will keep your portfolio manageable. As long as you use well-developed buy and sell guidelines, a smaller diversification can be just as profitable, if not more, than having thirty, forty, or fifty stocks giving you smaller, incremental returns.

Dollar Cost Averaging

This is easy to do if you have $50,000 or more to put into the market at one time. You can pick and choose your stocks and buy into whatever stocks you want. But if you're a person with a limited amount of cash on hand to get started, you may find it hard to pick and choose which stocks to invest in.

Now, more than ever before, buying stocks over time can be easily done, even if you only have a few dollars to get started. Many broker sites like Robinhood.com, Stockpile.com, and even larger brokerage companies like Charles Schwab and E-Trade are now tailored to cater to the smaller investor, eliminating trading commissions and allowing you to purchase even a fraction of a share if needed.

You can accumulate your shares over time by setting up a regular purchase plan, adding the same amount to your account every week, month, or year. This is pretty much the way your employer buys your shares of stocks in their employee plans. You can set the amount you want to invest on a regular basis and automatically purchase your shares accordingly.

One of the advantages of dollar cost averaging is that it evens out the price of each share. While one week the price may be a certain amount and the next time, it may be 10% higher or lower. This way, you never pay the highest or the lowest amount for each share of stock.

This plan does not work well for everyone nor does it work well for every stock. However, it is an option that allows you the option to get into the market much sooner, diversify your portfolio, and start earning a return much faster.

Accumulating stock is not the only reason you might not want to buy all your stocks at one time. By spreading out the purchases, adding a little at a time, you can still capitalize on market movements. If you're buying a particular stock at one price and then later, notice the price movements looked favorable, you could always add more to your portfolio. If you do this just make sure that the average cost of your different buys do not exceed a reasonable price so that you can still make a profit in the end.

How Long Should You Hold 'Em

Many new investors are caught up in the debate over long or short-term investing. Some advisors are quick to say you should ride it out until you get the price you want, and others will tell you to get in or out when the price is right.

The reason there is such a disparity between the two opinions is that it is a matter of investment style. What one person may be comfortable with may not be what you are comfortable with.

And in the end, the real answer is not how long you should hold them because that will depend on the movements of the market. The real issue is if you bought the right stock, to begin with.

If you've done your research and prepared well for your investment, the time you hold the stock should not matter. As long as you follow the guidelines in your choice, the market will dictate when you need to get in and out of a trade. Some stocks will fare better on the long-haul while others will do well with the short-term strategy. Each stock is different and your decision to move will be determined by its own dynamics.

A Word About IPOs – Are They Worth It?

When it comes to diversifying your portfolio, you'll find that you have plenty of options besides just buying stocks. We've already talked about the index and mutual funds, independent stocks, and penny stocks but there are a lot more options to choose from. You don't have to limit your portfolio to these. There are many alternative investment instruments to choose from.

Initial Public Offerings are an option that seems to attract the eye of many new investors. They are often more appealing to those who do not have a lot of money to invest in. Everyone wants to get in on the ground floor of the next big thing. Who wouldn't want to be a fly on the wall when Google, Amazon, or Microsoft offered their first IPO?

Unfortunately, these kinds of finds are few and far between. While profitable deals can be found, the odds of finding one are limited. You will also have to deal with a number of restrictions. Some IPOs have restrictions on how soon you could sell if the business doesn't do well, which could leave you vulnerable. You may not be able to exit your position when you need to and end up going down with the ship.

Also, many IPOs start off underpriced in an effort to encourage more buys. This shoots up the price on the first day or two of trading, but then you will see a drastic drop that they cannot recover from.

It is difficult to gauge how well they will perform since they have no history of research. There is no way to tell their true value or potential. For the new investor, IPOs may not be worth the added challenges that accompany them. This doesn't mean that you can't purchase an IPO if you have the stomach for it but as investing in the stock market is already a risky venture for a newcomer; it is an area of the market that may best be set aside until you have accumulated more experience.

If you are looking for other instruments to diversify your portfolio, it would be better to look at the myriad of alternatives available to you. Consider convertible bonds, tax shelters, warrants, mergers, FOREX, penny stocks, futures, and the like. Many of those are much safer than the IPOs and can still allow you to enter the market and make the kind of returns that can help you build your wealth.

Conclusion

The next step is to apply everything that you have learned. Investing in the stock market can be an interesting journey. Be ready to face some challenges along the way. The important thing is to keep on learning. Take note that to learn the strategies in this book, you have to practice them. Investing in stocks is just like learning a new skill. It does take some time and effort, but it is very much worth it. Again, do not rush the development process. The more that you learn, the more that you can minimize your losses and increase your profits.

If you want to achieve financial freedom or simply want to increase your income, then this book is for you. Investing in stocks can be challenging, but it is full of rewards for those who take the time and effort to learn it. There are people out there who earn their full-time income simply by investing in stocks. If you want a successful life by being your own boss, then give this wonderful opportunity a try.

Feel free to review this book and make your own reflections and modifications. Remember, you are dealing with a live and continuously moving market, so it is only right that you always strive for continuous improvement. This book has given you the tools to achieve total financial freedom. It is up to you to turn your newfound knowledge into actual practice.!

Thank you very much for the time you took to get through this book. If you made it this far, it is because you are serious about investing. Also, you are serious about making some real money.

You might still have some questions about what we covered in this book, and that's fair, as this topic is quite extensive. Nevertheless, I would encourage you to go over any section you feel you need to brush up on.

Also, I would be more than happy to assist you in clearing up any doubts you may still have about any topic in this book. Bear in mind that becoming proficient in stock market investing is a question of time and experience.

So, it's important to get those flight hours under your belt. You can do this by opening a practice account on a trading platform, in order to gain experience on a real-life simulator. In addition, you can gain valuable experience by starting off small and building you way up.

In a manner of speaking, it's like going to a casino figuring you're going to lose some money as you figure out the ins and outs of the game. Ultimately, stock market investing is just like a casino. If you don't know what you are doing, you will be guessing most of the time. That will only set you up for losses. But, if you know what you are doing, you will have a very good chance to make some money. You might even make more money than you ever thought possible.

As such, I would like to thank you once again for reading my book. I know that there are plenty of other options out there, so I hope that you leave a comment for other folks who may not know where to start. Your honest opinion will certainly help them figure out which book is right for them. I am sure that they will find as much value in this book as you did.

I wish you all the best in your endeavors. I am sure that, with a little time and effort, you will become a successful investor very soon.

Happy investing!

www.ingramcontent.com/pod-product-compliance
Lightning Source LLC
Chambersburg PA
CBHW071353210526
45465CB00001B/73